READINGS FOR WRITERS
Vol. II

KENYON*review*

READINGS FOR WRITERS
Vol. II

David H. Lynn, Editor

Copyright © *Kenyon Review*, 2017.

All rights reserved. No part of this book may be reproduced in any form or by any electronic or mechanical means including information storage and retrieval systems — except in the case of brief quotations embodied in critical articles or reviews — without the permission in writing from its publisher, the *Kenyon Review*.

Published by the *Kenyon Review*
Finn House, 102 West Wiggin St., Gambier, Ohio 43022
(740) 427-5208
Fax: (740) 427-5417
www.kenyonreview.org

Cover design and artwork by Stella Ryan-Lozon

ISBN: 978-1-883840-00-6

KENYON*review*

Readings for Writers
Volume 2

Cara Blue Adams *I Met Loss the Other Day*	
Winter 2009, Vol. 31, No. 1	1
M. Shahid Alam *Two Versions of a Ghazal from Ghalib*	
Winter 2013, KROnline	4
W. H. Auden *The Duet*	
Autumn 1947, Old Series Vol. 9, No. 4	6
Reginald Dwayne Betts *Crimson*	
Spring 2013, Vol. 35, No. 2	8
Eavan Boland *To Memory*	
Spring 2007, Vol. 29, No. 2	10
Cooper Lee Bombardier *A Trans Body's Path in Eight Folds*	
Summer 2016, KROnline	12
Jericho Brown *The Rest We Deserve*	
Summer 2012, Vol. 34, No. 3	16
Bonnie Jo Campbell *My Sister is in Pain*	
Fall 2015, KROnline	17
Rachel Cantor *Dead Dresses*	
Jan/Feb 2015, Vol. 37, No. 1	18
Mahmoud Darwish *Don't Write History as Poetry*	
Translated from Arabic by Fady Joudah	
Summer 2005, Vol. 27, No. 3	29
Don DeLillo *Coming Sun. Mon. Tues.*	
Summer 1966, Old Series, Vol. 28, No. 3	30
Brian Doyle *No*	
Spring 2008, Vol. 30, No. 2	34
Camille T. Dungy *Trophic Cascade*	
May/June 2015, Vol. 37, No. 3	44
Helen Forman *Ophelia*	
Spring 1951, Old Series, Vol. 13, No. 2	45
Joanna Goodman *Beginning with a Line from NPR*	
Winter 2005, Vol. 27, No. 1	46

Linda Gregerson *Cranes on the Seashore* Winter 2001, Vol. 23, No. 1	48
Kimiko Hahn *Circles and Breasts* Winter 2014, KROnline	51
Githa Hariharan *Diablo Baby* Fall 2008, Vol. 30, No. 4	52
Bob Hicok *How Origami Was Invented* Spring 1999, Vol. 21, No. 2	56
Alice Hoffman *The Witch of Truro* Spring 2004, Vol. 26, No. 2	58
Randall Jarrell *The Winter's Tale* Winter 1939, Old Series, Vol. 1, No. 1	67
Allison Joseph *Barbie's Little Sister* Spring 1996, Vol. 18, No. 2	70
Fady Joudah *Ladies and Gentlemen* Winter 2007, Vol. 29, No. 1	72
Konstantinos Kavaphes *Waiting for the Barbarians* Translated from Greek by Richmond Lattimore Spring 1955, Old Series, Vol. 17, No. 2	74
Brigit Pegeen Kelly *Dead Doe: I* Summer 1991, Vol. 13, No. 3	76
Brad Kessler *One Reader's Digest* Spring 2005, Vol. 27, No. 2	79
Colleen Kinder *One Bright Case of Idiopathic Cranofacial Erythema* Summer 2008, KROnline	95
Rickey Laurentiis *Lord and Chariot* Summer 2014, Vol. 36, No. 3	108
Robert Lowell *The Infinite* Autumn 1961, Old Series, Vol. 23, No. 4	110
Jamaal May *The Sky, Now Black with Birds* Summer 2013, Vol. 35, No. 3	111
W. S. Merwin *Under the Day* Winter 2002, Vol. 24, No. 1	113
Philip Metres *The Iraqi Curator's PowerPoint* Fall 2013, KROnline	114
Heather Monley *Town of Birds* Winter 2014, Vol. 36, No. 1	116

Marianne Moore *A Glass-Ribbed Nest*	
Summer 1940, Old Series, Vol. 2, No. 3	119
Diana Khoi Nguyen *Getting the Hero to Speak*	
Winter 2015, KROnline	121
Flannery O'Connor *The Life You Save May Be Your Own*	
Spring 1953, Old Series, Vol. 15, No. 2	122
Matthew Olzmann *In the Gallery of American Violence*	
Winter 2011, Vol. 33, No. 1	133
Lucia Perillo *Wild Birds Unlimited*	
Winter 2012, KROnline	134
Carl Phillips *Radiance Versus Ordinary Light*	
Spring 2005, Vol. 27, No. 2	136
Sylvia Plath *The Beekeeper's Daughter*	
Autumn 1960, Old Series, Vol. 21, No. 4	137
D. A. Powell *Calling All Gods*	
Spring 2013, Vol. 35, No. 2	138
John Crowe Ransom *Winter Remembered*	
From *Selected Poems*, Third Edition 1969	139
Theodore Roethke *A Light Breather*	
Summer 1950, Old Series, Vol. 12, No. 3	140
Onnesha Roychoudhuri *Where I'm Writing From*	
Winter 2016, KROnline	141
Muriel Rukeyser *Eyes of Night-Time*	
Spring 1947, Old Series, Vol. 9, No. 2	150
Rion Amilcar Scott *Three Insurrections*	
May/June 2016, Vol. 38, No. 3	151
Solmaz Sharif *Desired Appreciation*	
Jan/Feb 2016, Vol. 38, No. 1	166
Wallace Stevens *Variations on a Summer Day*	
Winter 1940, Old Series, Vol. 2, No. 1	168
Mark Strand *Anywhere Could Be Somewhere;*	
Not To Miss The Great Thing	
Winter 2012, KROnline	172
Virgil Suárez *Arroz*	
Winter 1999, Vol. 21, No. 1	173
Arthur Sze *Sight Lines*	
May/June 2015, Vol. 37, No. 3	175
Mary Szybist *Girls Overheard While Assembling a Puzzle*	
Fall 2011, Vol. 33, No. 4	177

Sam Taylor *[Wikipedia, or the Late Style of Orpheus]*
   May/June 2016, Vol. 38, No. 3   179

Dylan Thomas *Poem*
   Summer 1939, Old Series, Vol. 1, No. 3   181

Patrick Tobin *Cake*
   Winter 2007, Vol. 29, No. 1   183

Phillip B. Williams *Luminous, Whatever Honey*
   Jan/Feb 2016, Vol. 38, No. 1   196

James Wright *All the Beautiful Are Blameless*
   Autumn 1958, Old Series, Vol. 20, No. 4   197

Charles Wyatt *From* The Spirit Autobiography of S. M. Jones
   Winter 2003, Vol. 25, No. 1   199

Javier Zamora *To Abuelita Nelly*
   May/June 2016, Vol. 38, No. 3   205

Rachel Zucker *Just off the Road near Lynchburg, Virginia*
   Summer 2013, Vol. 35, No. 3   206

Cara Blue Adams
2008 Kenyon Review Short Fiction Contest Winner

I Met Loss the Other Day

I met Loss the other day. I took his measurements. My yellow tape looped around my arm, pins held tight between my pursed lips, I circled him. I measured his thin wrists, his frail neck, his elegantly sloped shoulders. Inseam, sleeve length, the stretch of his forearm, I marked them down in pencil.

He was small. He stood very still as I worked.

His entourage, six thick-necked men, boisterous despite their size, pale handkerchiefs peeking from their dark suits' breast pockets, poked in the nooks and crannies of my shop. They hula-hooped with my skirt wires, nudged one another with my dead mother's ornate wood-handled umbrella, tossed fabric bolts back and forth. Loss looked straight ahead, glancing over only when a crash erupted or someone called to him affectionately.

No one used his name. To them, he was Oss, Lossie, Bonedaddy.

Loss wanted a single-breasted suit, standard issue, merino wool and cashmere with a peaked lapel, but also a prayer robe and a felt cloak. He was going on holiday, he told me. Where, he didn't say.

He produced a tailor's pattern book from 1589. I turned the dry pages. Cutting patterns for clerical robes, silk kirtles, ropa de letrado, all given in ells. One ell equals forty-five inches: this is ancestral knowledge, parceled with the family Bible and shears, passed down the years from grandfather to father, father to son. Loss didn't know this. He handed me a conversion table.

"A Savile Row tailor threw me out," he told me.

I told Loss I could give him what he wanted. Ducking the pincushions that whizzed by my head, I flipped through my notebook to a blank page and noted his figuration and posture. I asked him to stand relaxed. He nodded but remained stiff.

As I sketched, I asked Loss about his operation.

Hundreds of people were in his employ, Loss told me. Cataloguing, mostly. Rows of dark heads with neat parts bent over typewriters, clacking away.

"You can't imagine the clamor," he said. "Eventually it numbs you."

Worse, Loss said, were the administrative meetings. The ceaseless bickering over what constituted loss. Keys, located after four panicky minutes: lost or just misplaced? A silver dollar stolen from an aunt's purse and tossed down a wishing well, a swallowed tooth, an uncle in the grasp of dementia. How are we to gauge? The problems of classification were endless and unyielding.

As he spoke, I saw the warehouses. Each person's losses filed in long skinny drawers. The cavernous echo of clerks' footsteps as they pushed ladders to the far reaches. Each birth a long span of empty drawer that filled. Slow or quick, it always filled.

Each time someone died, Loss told me, the records were purged. In the night, bonfires dotted the perimeter.

I finished. We discussed drape and cut, scheduled a second fitting. Loss offered to pay in cash. Half up front, half after the skeleton baste. His money roll was enormous. He peeled away crisp hundreds like onion skins.

"No need to pay the second half," I told him. Loss raised an eyebrow.

"Have a clerk pull my note cards," I said. "I'll take those instead."

Loss shook his head. Beneath his eyes were tiny plum veins. "They'd fill a wheelbarrow. Take the money. Buy something. Only in Vegas can you trade with your losses."

I hefted the heavy felt in my hands. Loss reached out and stroked it. I waited. He said nothing.

I waited some more.

"Okay," Loss said finally, "but just a sampling. And duplicates only." We shook.

After he left, I oiled my shears. I marked the thin brown-speckled pattern paper with Loss's measurements. Scotch-taped to the window, the paper shone like stained glass. In my hands, the fabric came apart and then together again in Loss's shape. Not alchemy, but close, I thought. Close.

At the appointed hour, Loss returned. His entourage waited outside, kicking empty cans into the gutter. In the gray light they looked at once thuggish and impossibly young.

During the fitting, Loss was patient. He stretched out his arms like a child playing airplane, reached for the sky, ducked and feinted. A few minor adjustments were agreed upon, but everything fit him beautifully.

I promised him the finished garments sewn up tight as a shroud in ten days' time. Loss nodded, said his assistant would collect them, and then reached inside his jacket and handed me three manila cards.

Each card was annotated in an old-fashioned typeface. My name appeared at the top left, the series number at the top right. Dead center was the list. *Gold filling*, the first card began. *Train schedule. Yellow slicker just before the sky opened. Bearings (ball). Bearings (sense of). Orange rind. Tax forms.*

Things I couldn't remember losing. Things I'd missed all my life.

"Sure you don't want the money?" Loss asked. "You could buy another slicker."

"No thanks," I said.

Loss shrugged. I had the sense he'd seen it before: people unwilling to let go of what was gone.

Before he let himself out, Loss brushed my cheek lightly with the back of his knuckles — just the way you always would. Just the way I know you will again, after you walk barefoot down the dirt drive to your mailbox, slit open my envelope and find these cards, after you finally hold in your hand what for all those years I could never bring myself to show you.

M. Shahid Alam

Two Versions of a Ghazal from Ghalib

Ghalib, pen name of Mirza Asadullah Khan, a poet of nineteenth-century India, wrote in Urdu and Persian. He is widely regarded as the greatest poet of the Urdu language.

I

You say I cannot have it if you find my heart.
It was once mine: now I know who has it.

Love is by far the best thing in life. It took
All my sorrows: but has me hooked to it.

She is coy & cunning, sweet, exacting too.
She is playing you when you do not know it.

The heart can tell its story: what *I* know is this,
Every time I look for it, you say you have it.

My mentor likes to rub salt in my wounds.
Sir Tormentor, I ask, what do you take from it?

II

She keeps a store for hearts lost and stolen.
Should I lose one I know where to look for it.

Life's longest epic is a day in love. I gave up
All my cares for one that takes no cure.

In life, she is laid back, in love enigmatic.
What if she plays cool, she is aching for you.

For many years now, I have polished this heart.
I will get its value when she puts a price on it.

I know you like to rub salt in my wounds.
This cauterizes me: what does it do for you?

W. H. Auden

The Duet

    All winter long the huge sad lady
Sang to her warm house of the heart betrayed: —
    Love lies delirious and a-dying;
The purlieus are shaken by his sharp cry.
    But back across the fret dividing
His wildernesses from her floral side
    All winter long a scrunty beggar
With one glass eye and one hickory leg,
    Stumping about half-drunk through stony
Ravines and over dead volcanic cones,
    Refused her tragic hurt, declaring
A happy passion to the freezing air,
    Turning his barrel-organ, playing
Lanterloo my lovely, my First-of-May.

    Louder on nights when in cold glory
The full moon made its meditative tour,
    To big chords from her black grand piano
She sang the disappointment and the fear
    For all her lawns and orchards: — *Slowly*
The spreading ache bechills the rampant glow
    Of fortune-hunting blood; Time conjures
The moskered ancestral tower to plunge
    From its fastidious cornice down to
The pigsties far below; the oaks turn brown;
    The cute little botts of the sailors
Are snapped up by the sea. But to her gale
    Of sorrow from the moonstruck darkness
The ragged runagate opposed his spark,

      For still his scrannel music-making
In tipsy joy across the gliddered lake,
      Praising for all the rocks and craters
The green refreshments of the watered state,
      Cried nonsense to her large repining:
The windows have opened; a royal wine
      Is poured out for the subtle pudding
Light industry is humming in the wood;
      The bluebirds bless us from the fences;
We know the time and where to find our friends.

Reginald Dwayne Betts

Crimson

When they found his body today,
All forty-seven of his years drowned
In a pool he paid for with blood, I thought
Of my brother. He has life. And Rodney
King's head was cracked open before a live
Audience. This is 1991 and the Bad Boys
From Detroit are in the Finals again, or will be
When June comes around and all around me shatters.
They say King had fifty-nine fractures, bones brittle,
Brittle after that night when he became
Why every young dude I knew screamed "Fuck
The Police." We only cursed what could kill us.
The day blood washed over the freshest pair of Timbs
On a Richmond street; those batons slam dancing
On King's head; my father's weary eyes; and
The money, all those thousands we spent trying
To resurrect a dead man with an appeal,
The millions spent making Rodney King rise again.
His name, my brother's, is Juvenile, or Juvie — but
No longer Christopher. This is what he tells me
The men he breaks bread with call him. Or called
Him, a dozen years ago, before he, too, became
An old head, veteran of count time and shakedowns.
It's how they christen niggas who own their first
Cell before sixteen — and because King took that ass
Whupping four days before cuffs clanked around
Christopher's wrist the first time, back when he
Was what they call "on the run." When the news
Came on, and we caught it halfway through, just
Listening as we sweated the phone for news,

We thought it was my brother crouched under blows
And bleeding like a dog in them streets.
And even now we confuse the two events.

Eavan Boland

To Memory

This is for you, goddess that you are.
This is a record for us both, this is a chronicle.
There should be more of them, they should be lyrical
and factual, and true, they should be written down
and spoken out on rainy afternoons, instead of which
they fall away; so I have written this, so it will not.
My last childless winter was the same
as all the other ones. Outside my window
the motherless landscape hoarded its own kind.
Light fattened the shadows; frost harried the snowdrops.
There was a logic to it, the way my mother loved astrology —
she came from a valley in the country
where everything that was haphazard and ill-timed
about our history had happened and so it seemed natural
that what she wanted most were the arts of the predetermined.
My child was born at the end of winter. How to prove it?
Not the child, of course, who slept in pre-spring darkness,
but the fact that the ocean — moonless, stripped of current —
entered the room quietly one evening and
lay down in the weave of the rug, and could be seen
shifting and sighing in blue-green sisal and I said
nothing about it, then or later, to anyone and when
the spring arrived I was ready to see a single field in
the distance on the Dublin hills allow its heathery color
to detach itself and come upstairs and settle in
the corner of the room furthest from the window.
I could, of course, continue. I could list for you
a whole inventory of elements and fixed entities
that broke away and found themselves disordered in
that season, its unruly happenstance, without

a thought for laws that until then had barred
an apple flower from opening at midnight
or lilac rooting in the coldest part of the ocean. Then
it stopped. Little by little what was there came back.
Slowly at first; then surely. I realized what had happened
was secret, hardly possible, to be remembered always,
which is why you are listening as rain comes down
restored to its logic, responsive to air and land
and I am telling you this: you are after all
not simply the goddess of memory, you have
nine daughters yourself and can understand.

Cooper Lee Bombardier

A Trans Body's Path in Eight Folds

"Thou wast not born for death, immortal Bird! No hungry generations tread thee down."
 —John Keats "Ode to a Nightingale"

One: right concentration

A trans body sightsees at Carlsbad Caverns. It pays admission and enters the gap-toothed maw. Eyes are open but not working at first, seeing only the green opposite of the hot white outside. Soon, the trans eyes forget the world's way of seeing in favor of its own vision in the cool balm of dark. It feels a kinship with the stalactites fanging down from the dark ribbed roof, growing and changing ever so slowly, drip by drip. An inch a century if that. The waiting and the long unfolding to *become*, molecule by molecule. In the yellowing glow of a miner's headlamp, the trans body spelunks toward nature's confirmation of the impossible made manifest, and vows to cultivate the patience of a cave.

Two: right action

A trans body visits a lover in a high desert town in the American Southwest. While running — near to panting from altitude — on a community center treadmill, this trans body spots another trans body on an adjacent treadmill two machines over. A wash of warm recognition floods the one at the sight of another. The trans body runs in place and listens to punk rock through headphones while shaping a way to connect with the other trans body. *Hello*, it imagines saying, *me, too.* Or: *I am your people.* Too stiff? Too awkward? *I am so happy you and I are here together in this place of all places. How many more of us might be here?* Slowing the treadmill down to run-tripping on the flapping black rubber belt, the trans body knows it cannot make any reach toward the other. More likely than a welcomed connection, it could be received as an affront, a highlighting of some failure of detail, or worse, a dangerous positioning of crosshairs on the back of the other. One trans body might go undetected, but two trans bodies begin to shape an identifiable pattern. Two trans bodies dismount treadmills, sweating, alone.

Three: right speech
A trans body meets another trans body for coffee. In the span of drinking a twelve ounce Americano, one trans body is smudged out and rendered invisible by the other. Countless people wield the power to erase a trans body, but nothing wounds to the same extent as when it happens by the hands of another trans body. A trans body rents a place with a friend. The friend leans on the trans body sometimes as if they were spouses or two old trees bordering a field who fell into each other in a windstorm; hard to tell who is holding the other up. The friend sometimes shakes out tired assumptions about "X" or "Y" like wet wash about to be pinned to a line that only extends in two finite directions. One day the friend-spouse directs the trans body to do something in a highly divided public space. When the trans body reminds the housemate-friend why this suggested action would not be ideal, how it would expose, embarrass, or worse — imperil a trans body, the spousemate says: *sometimes I forget you are trans*, sharp with darts of exasperation like the trans body's transness is the most difficult thing in the world for the housemate (and friend) to bear, and yet the easiest thing in the world to forget.

Four: right view
A trans body is denoted "A" at birth but by surviving over half a lifetime of social misadventures, zigzagging rat-maze bureaucracy, hustling the system, defying critics and naysayers huddled around smoldering embers of damp fires in all worn camps, performing emotional sorcery, the application of rudimentary medical technology, and a highly-honed ability to charm service workers and gatekeeping personnel at each level of the salt-sea lock, is able to exist in relative comfort as "B." This trans body's ability to live as "B" magnetizes to itself praise and blame in equal and alternating currents. This trans body's comfort in inhabiting "B" does not stand as a referendum on "A," nor upon A1, A2, A3 ... B1, B2, ... nor does it deny the existence of "C." It simply feels like if it has to choose a climate — say, the sandstone hot dry desert or the gray-green damp pine woods — it chooses woods. The trans body still loves the desert for its own magic light, but a place only feels like home when it is home.

Five: right intention

A trans body telegraphs thinly coded messages out over the wire. The information is everywhere but the connections are fleeting when they are soldered together at all. Birds fly out with destinations imprinted in their minds and scrolls tied to their feet. Sometimes they land and other times never come home to roost, eliciting neither hope nor surprise. They do the work of gossip but are much cuter, albeit in an archaic way. The messenger birds are too troublesome for white urban middle-class young adults to co-opt. Far offshore there are other trans bodies bobbing like tiny ships in blueblack water, their little red lights blinking out: *I'm here, I'm here, I'm here. . . .* Within the empty shape of a few beats, a slower light arcs out from atop a rocky cliff, slicing the black water apart from the black sky like a cake, its beam refracted through the thick-scaled Fresnel prisms of the lighthouse lamp, in a brief whip and sweep away it answers back: *Alone, alone . . .* blink, sweep . . . *Alone, alone. . . .* On land the fallen are called bodies, but at sea the lost are called souls.

Six: right effort

A trans body goes to the low-cost clinic on indigent status and performs a show. The most complex and personal interstices of self and body are reduced to carved primary colored wooden blocks and ABCs. The trans body has been trans longer than the doctor has been a doctor. The teacher pretends to be a student. The trans body is a bad kid in school who says what you want to hear to avoid detention. This trans body trains the doctor to see it as a patient and its need as deserving of care much in the same way wolves once trained humans to see them as dogs.

Seven: right livelihood

A trans body lives and dies a young trans life within the cold blue frame of a screen. Another trans body takes shape in the late afternoon of midlife, confounding those around in concentric ripples that dissipate with distance. Ejected and unwanted; as burnt as toast from the chrome slots of society, a trans body walks a rain-soaked alley bearing a heavy bindle stiff as an exhausting punishment for noncompliance. One trans body bikes the bridge and stops at the midpoint to stare at the river below and listen for the call of sirens, while another trans body's fist connects with the jaw of a would-be attacker. Another trans body jostles past on a downtown sidewalk, unnoticed, while another stands at a podium, grasping a bronze trophy of recognition. A trans body cradles a child in tender arms. Despair and hope pulse through a trans body in equal measure. Beneath flesh, the bones of the trans body are as likely as the non-trans body to receive the frequency of either vibration — only the path of sound differs.

Eight: right mindfulness

The trans body asks for something so internal and deeply known to be named, something that longs for a witness in the clean light of day. The trans body asks for an expansion of what is perceived to be conceivable, to be included in the taxonomy of the "real." The human mind often discovers that what we thought to be one thing is indeed another, and that new knowledge is embraced with joy — Pluto is not a planet; we are a galaxy among countless others; we can listen to the sound of a comet streaking a fiery brushstroke across the silence of space; we can measure the code of our DNA against the matrix of the trees. Human hearts and imaginations swell at what is possible. A trans body asks that the wonder of the world *contains it* within all of the world's resplendent glory.

Jericho Brown

The Rest We Deserve

Our walls are thin, and the man who won't say hello
Back to me in the morning as we lock ourselves out
Of our homes — won't even nod my way as black men
Do when they see themselves in you — sings "Precious,
Precious," the only song he must know, to the newborn
Other neighbors tell me is all he has left of a woman
Who either died, went to rehab, or left him for another,
Depending on the fool telling the story and the time
Of day it gets told. I don't know why it bothers me.
I don't need him to love me the way he loves that child,
Pacing an apartment I imagine looks just like mine
With a baby in his arms, none of us allowed the rest
We deserve, him awful and off-key, her — is it a her? —
Shrill as any abandoned animal should be. I want
To hurt him, and I want to help. I think of knocking
To say he doesn't have to be polite to me, but he should
Try stuffing the kid in a drawer and closing it, or
Knocking to show him the magic made when you sit
An infant in a car seat on top of a washer while you do
A little late-night laundry. Why do I think he owes me,
That our knowledge of all the words to Jackie Moore's
One hit makes him mine enough not to mind the man
He sees me kiss good-bye while he rolls his eyes, a baby
Strapped to his back, a tie around his neck, and me
Yawning because she or my lover didn't let me sleep?
What is the name for the thing growing in the smallest
Of us when we open our mouths at odd hours and shriek?

Bonnie Jo Campbell

My Sister is in Pain

Unbearable pain when she gets up in the morning to go to work, when she goes to bed at night, and when she sleeps, she sleeps in pain and wakes up in pain again and dresses in her stretch-waist pants and bright complicated sweaters, heats up meals from packages, substitutes low-fat margarine for butter, sucralose for sugar, and smokes cigarettes in pain on her porch, while squirrels scramble like idiots up trees, and cars without mufflers vomit smoke and clatter through this neighborhood of potholes and broken windows, where kids steal anything to sell for money to buy meth. Her doctors shrug in their lab coats, send her to specialists who throw up their arms. Pain like airplanes with their airplane-engine noise, flying over and messing up the sky. Pain like dishes in the sink — not just her own dishes, but dishes of strangers who've left them there for days, in cold, gray water. She is our mother's daughter, but we don't know who she is or what her pain could mean, her cicadas of pain on summer nights, the jolts in her spine like flashes of abominable fireflies, pain that radiates from her intestines like the shocks of electric eels. Stabbing pain sixty hours a week as she bathes and medicates and tends to the needs and the pain of old ladies for minimum wage, throbbing pain when she has a day off. She was born more beautiful than the rest of us and called out more loudly from her crib, cried in her bed, and outside in the woods she wailed — she never said what those boys did to her beside the creek. Imagine a long corridor with hundreds of rooms all closed against pain; she walks down the corridor and her pain does not diminish. Whether or not she stops and knocks on any door, whether or not anyone invites her in for a cool drink, whether or not one of the people who invites her in for a cool drink is myself, still, her pain does not diminish. We rarely call her, are polite at Christmas, give tentative embraces, compliment her sweaters, her beads, and hair bows. We nod when she explains about her special shoes, her Copper Wear as seen on TV. The gifts she brings us are elaborately wrapped. We untie the ribbons in terror.

Rachel Cantor

Dead Dresses

It being an odd day, they meet on Emmilloni's bunk, Emmi being the odd one. Tomorrow, they meet on Anniloni's bunk, Anni being the even one. Brannilini, up top, is the leap year: look! he leaps bunk to bunk, how odd! He does this because Charlemeanie is at boarding school, abandoning her side of the top, abandoning them all to Papa's silences and Auntie's sewing hour. She writes excited letters: I'm learning Geography! I'm learning Arithmetic! As if hills and numbers were something to talk about.

In leaping, Branni slips and all but falls between the bunks. His leg dangles between them, already he's screaming, and not just because Emmi has taken a bite of his thigh.

When Papa sent Emmi to boarding school, she famously stopped eating.

I was more dead than alive, she explained to Anni. They had no choice but to send me home.

What she doesn't say: Papa couldn't afford to lose more daughters.

What was it like, almost dying, Anni asks, not for the first time.

It was very, very quiet, Emmi says. Every anomalous day, it was even quieter.

It sounds nice, Anni says. Everything quiet.

Emmi doesn't like it when Anni talks like that. You will never have to die, she says, because we will always be together. She squeezes Anni under the covers.

But if we weren't, Anni says, reasonably.

Oh, Emmi says.

Branni is still screaming.

..

The reasons Charloni is a meanie are self-evident:

She abandoned them.

She likes it where she is.

Where she is is very stupid, yet she likes it.

She tells everyone she likes it, she doesn't care whom she hurts.

She says she misses them, but if she did, she wouldn't be there, she'd be here.

She acts like they should want to go.

She writes them letters, but not often enough, and when she does, she writes about being *there*.

She thinks she's better than everyone, because she knows numbers and hills.

• •

Before they tell their tale, there are things Emmi and Anni must do:

They must show each other their roosters. They must touch each other's roosters, but only a tap. They must touch their tongues (three times). They must say magic words. This is done when Branni isn't around, for Branni is a boy, or it is done quietly, under the covers.

The rooster thing happens in the bathroom, where the girls pee together, despite Auntie's admonishments. Touching tongues happens under the covers.

Actually, they don't show their roosters anymore, not since Emmi started sprouting; soon she will be an animal, not a rooster.

The magic words happen in each other's ears.

• •

The sister is held captive in the evil Lord's dungeon, her hands clasped in irons above her head.

She groans wretchedly, says Emmi.

Yes, says Anni.

But no one can hear.

Except the imprisoned old man, remember? The one who gave away the secret of the castle when he was a boy. He has a beard down to his knees which covers his . . .

His choo-choo, I remember, but he's dead.

Oh, Anni says.

The sister doesn't have to look at that.

I've got a secret, Branni says from his bunk, casually, as if to himself.

The girls ignore him. They lie close together under the covers, Emmi's arm around Anni.

Evil Lord Castlering makes her take off her clothes, she whispers. He lets the servants look at her. He makes her show them her rooster.

Maybe her hair is long enough to cover that, Anni says.

No, says Emmi. This is when she cries abundantly.

Can the fairy godmother arrive? asks Anni.

There is no fairy godmother, Emmi says.

It's a really good secret, Branni says. If my sisters are nice to me, I might tell them.

The girls ignore him. The sister does not fare well in the dungeon of the evil Lord. Just when she thinks she's slipped free of her shackles, a blue servant dwarf arrives with a maggoty meal. Just when she's convinced the dwarf to release her, evil Lord Castlering arrives to laugh at her, and slice the dwarf in two.

This shall be your roommate, he guffaws. *Nay, your double roommate! Hahahahahaha!*

It is unclear what the sister has done to deserve this fate, except to be good and pure and otherwise deserving. The walls of the dungeon sweat drops of her tears.

If Branni were allowed to tell this story, he'd assemble great masses of soldiers with sharp and explosive weapons to storm the dungeon, draw, quarter, tar, and disembowel the evil Lord, and release the maiden to great fanfare. Charlemeanie would help, marrying the sister to the dashing Lieutenant LaGuardia. But Branni isn't allowed to tell the tale, and Meanie is away.

The secret has something to do with all of us, he says.

Go away, Emmi says.

. .

Emmi teaches Anni what it's like to be dead.

First you lie perfectly still. No — arms by your side. Yes, like that, touching nothing. Now you think about absolutely nothing. Go ahead, try.

The two girls lie perfectly still.

I keep thinking about thinking nothing, Anni says. Then I think about lunch.

Keep trying.

Anni keeps trying.

I don't think I can do it, she says.

It takes practice, Emmi says.

Can you do it? Anni asks.

Oh, yes, Emmi says.

Anni tries again, then scratches her nose, because she's thinking about lunch.

I think you'll find this is when a girl is most fine-looking, Emmi explains.

Is this what *they* looked like? Anni whispers. She knows not to say their names.

Oh, yes, Emmi says.

I remember, Anni says, though she doesn't.

You're always going to be ugly, Branni says from above, especially when you're dead.

The girls ignore him, thinking about nothing.

Because that's when worms crawl inside and out of your nose.

• •

The sister by now has escaped — she's riding the moors on a handsome black stallion, who likes to rear on his hind legs and roar. They haven't decided yet if he can fly, because they're not sure where the sister has to go. For now, it's enough that she gallops on the moors. Under the moonlight. In a white dress she found on a clothesline, or else she'd be nude.

Emmi and Anni take a break from their tale.

My hair is longer, Emmi says, but yours is curlier. That makes us even.

She fingers Anni's curls, and her own frizzy locks.

Anni nods.

And I'm taller.

But you're older, Anni says.

I will always be older, Emmi says.

Anni nods.

So really, I'm ahead there, Emmi says. I'm even taller than Charlemeanie, and she's older than everyone, so I think I win on tallness.

My eyes are violet, Anni says.

My eyes have no color, Emmi says.

They're gray.

That's no color. So we're even there.

You're both toadstools, Branni says from above, and he throws his pillow onto them.

Emmi snickers and puts the pillow behind their heads.

Hey, give me back my pillow! Branni yells. Give it back! Give it back!

You'll have to come get it, Emmi says, and you wouldn't dare.

Emmi's right: he wouldn't dare.

• •

They plan what to do when Charlemeanie comes back for the holidays.

Will we call her Charlemeanie? Anni asks.

Always, Emmi says.

Even to her face?

To her face we'll call her Your Fourteen-Year-Old Royal Greatness, Your Most High and Mighty Aloofness, Your Royal Higher-than-High Who-Cares-About-Your-Snootiest Snootness. We shall say, Tell us about your hills and numbers, and then we shall fall asleep.

Emmi laughs.

I miss Charli, Anni says.

Charlemeanie.

Charlemeanie.

Well, she doesn't miss us. She's happy without us, remember?

Will she die at school?

The others died at school, she knows. Emmi almost died at school.

Charlemeanie will never die. She'll outlive us all. She's not beautiful enough to die.

You guys are ugly artichokes, Branni says, and I'll never tell you my secret.

• •

When Papa and the three go on an excursion to the park, Branni walks with Papa, while the girls dally behind in their white dresses, arms entwined. In their minds they carry parasols; servants tend to the pugs; swains wait upon every curve, hoping to toss waistcoats onto puddles so they'll not soil their Mary Janes. They ignore the swains, for none is handsome or rich enough for princesses like them. Papa and Branni discuss Current Events, while Emmi and Anni note the arrival, over the horizon, of the demon Ahasuerus holding a scepter of fire and snakes, flanked by three dozen of his grisliest flesh-eating giants, their arms outstretched. . . .

Anni screams!

• •

When Charlemeanie comes home for the holidays, she must win Emmi over — with praises, special invitations, cajoling. You're looking taller, but, she says, catching the look in Emmi's eye, but not too tall, just the right height, for right now. She uses pocket money to buy Emmi gifts: a locket, which Emmi returns, saying she prefers valuable metals and costly stones. She asks to see Emmi's stories, which Emmi refuses, saying they belong to girls who stay at home. She offers to teach them about hills and numbers, but Emmi laughs. Before long, Charlemeanie heads back to school, looking over her shoulder to see if Emmi waves (she does not). Branni gives her a bear hug and they knock brains, the better to mingle them; Papa gives her a handkerchief, Aunt gives practical advice. Anni cries all night. Emmi says maybe she should join Charlemeanie at school, where surely she'd die.

• •

Branni does have a secret, and it's so big, he doesn't know how to tell it.

• •

Neither Emmi nor Anni has outgrown Auntie's sewing hour. After tea but before supper they sew clothes for the poor, often by mending Anni's outgrown dresses, which have been passed from sister to sister, and are barely white, despite assiduous application of bleach. Some are so old they originated in the oldest sisters, whose names are not mentioned, which causes Anni to consider them *dead dresses*.

Since Emmi became bigger than Charlemeanie, she has taken to labeling her dresses, so Charli should remember whence they came, once they come to her. Property of Queen Emmi, she writes in marker inside the collar, so darkly it can be read in red reverse around Charlemeanie's neck, a palimpsest bled into muslin.

Also they sew rag dolls for the poor, out of linens that cannot be saved. Anni has become adept at sewing doll hems, for her eyes are fine.

I thought *we* were poor, Anni says.

Hush, Aunt says. We are in *straightened circumstances*. You don't see anyone giving us rag dolls, do you?

Anni shakes her head.

You always had a rag doll of your own, didn't you?

Anni nods.

Before they may enter Aunt's doubly heated room (for she maintains two space heaters to keep off the chill), they must submit to inspection. Dirt behind the ear, she says, has dashed many a match. As often as not, Emmi is sent to scrub her fingernails.

While they sew, Aunt talks about comportment and family history. Emmi nods as if listening, but in fact she imagines the sisters — there are two of them now, surrounded by evil-looking men in torn-up clothing, raggedy men with half-grown whiskers and whiskey breath, who whistle and whisper things the girls do not understand. As the men sidle closer, stinking of tobacco and bad deeds, their necks sweating, their teeth broken and brown, the girls clasp hands, murmuring each other's names. They would rather die than be taken! But taken where? Emmi doesn't know. It's not a dungeon where girls are taken, it's not a place, really — it's a state of being brought about by time in which girls *change*. Emmi has seen it — not in her own family, of course, but in their building, where she watches everything (sometimes on the fire escape, aka the golden ladder, her seeing-eye glass hidden by a floppy hat); she has seen girls change, ferocious girls who used to beat Emmi for standing on the wrong side of the pavement. They *simper* now, hobbling on stilted shoes. Men's ruling desire is the ruination of women, Aunt has said (and Emmi has no reason to doubt her, for Papa ruined their mother, and he is the best man in the world), but what she doesn't understand is why women consent — why they rush to ruination, simpering and hobbling! Her own sisters, older than she, had chosen to die rather than face this ordeal. Emmi hopes to find an easier way.

I shall never marry, Emmi announces, interrupting Aunt, who has been explaining the several ways in which ladies might circumspectly prevent food from lingering betwixt their teeth.

You'll change your mind, Aunt says, accustomed to Emmi's non sequiturs — truthfully, she has hope only for Anni.

I never change my mind, says Emmi.

Aunt nods, then motions to see Emmi's rag doll. Its facial expression is frightening: two lopsided eyes and a crazy smile, sewn shut with cross-stitching.

You shall not make of yourself a seamstress, either, Aunt says, and commences to unravel the face.

• •

The girls discuss words. Hair is *tresses*, or *golden locks*. A forehead is always a *brow*; when possible, it should be *clear*. A dress is always a *gown*, never a *frock*. There is no good name for bosoms, or roosters, or belly-bottoms: these should not appear in stories, not any more.

• •

Branni has traveled seven hours to see Charli.

She looks very well, he says from the bunk above.

The girls ignore him, whispering under the covers. The sisters have concocted a plot, and it is daring: they shall set fire to the place where the ragged men congregate, after ensuring that all are closed within.

She still doesn't know as much as I, says Branni. For example, about Latin or Greek. I have quizzed her on the Peloponnesian War, and have ascertained this for certain.

The sisters are about to light the flame, but they are stopped by Lieutenant LaGuardia, who argues in favor of another punishment: the men shall be stripped of their land holdings, for in fact, they are quite wealthy, being the forgotten sons of the world's richest man. These holdings shall go to the sisters so they might build a fortress; LaGuardia shall help them, if they but spare the men.

She was very pleased with the stories I showed her, Branni says. I could show them to you, if you wanted. One is illustrated quite nicely with dragon guards and artillery.

The sisters hold the lighted match and consider the pros and cons.

• •

One of the sisters falls in love.

Emmi is white-faced as she decides this.

Not with one of the scraggly men, no, not with LaGuardia — with a different man.

What's the other sister to do? Anni asks, concerned.

The man is the long-lost son of the Emperor of Light, the one who was kidnapped as a child by the Monster of the Everglades, remember?

I don't, Anni says.

The monster wanted all the world's light, and twenty years later, the Emperor was still gathering it as ransom.

Anni looks blank.

It was a long time ago, Emmi says. He's spent all these twenty years finding his way industriously back to the moors, having escaped at the age of six. He's had multiple adversaries since then.

Like who?

It doesn't matter. What's important is that when he emerges from the forest, a ray of light catches his countenance, and the sheen of sweat on his arms, alerting the girls to his ominous presence.

I think he's very handsome, Anni says.

Emmi is silent a moment, then nods.

In a flash of an instant, the man . . .

Whose name is Ashwell!

Whose name is . . . Philip the Strong, falls in love with Betsy-Serena, the younger sister. But tragically at that very moment, the elder, Marina-Helena, falls in love with him, for he is dark with chestnut curls, and his expression is superior, and he can fight an entire army. She faints, of course, but Philip doesn't tend to her, he sees only Betsy-Serena, who kneels to her sister's aid.

Oh, says Anni. Oh, no, she says. Does this mean they have to die?

This means they have to die, Emmi says.

• •

Branni offers to share his newest toy — a machine gun that can wipe out an entire garrison at forty miles.

Come on! he says. It's better than your stupid dolls!

Emmi and Anni's rag dolls sit at the edge of their bunks, attending to the story. Each wears a placid expression. Neither is bothered when Branni murders them with his gun.

• •

The girls are preparing for the wedding of Philip the Strong and Betsy-Serena, only Marina-Helena has plans to hand her sister over to evil Lord Castlering, who has been looking for her, hunting her with slavering dogs. Marina-Helena will then substitute herself for her sister. Philip the Strong will think she is Betsy-Serena, because she will be wearing her sister's dress.

Branni is dropping papers from his latest story onto their heads, complete with realistic illustrations of the latest Glasstown massacre, sixty rebels dead, their fingers severed and worn, sewn together, around the heads of the victors.

The rag dolls are to be maids of honor. They are too stupid, Emmi says, to recognize the substitution.

Look! Branni shouts. I can write with both hands! and he drops more papers, which Emmi bats to the side.

Anni is not certain about this turn of events, as the sisters have always had each other and now what do they have, but she trusts Emmi.

Branni is roaring in his bunk.

Shut up, penguin! Emmi shouts.

I can't help it, he says. The lions have gotten loose! *ROARRR!*

• •

You're like Betsy-Serena, Emmi says.

Because I'm younger?

Younger, and prettier. Marina-Helena is very tall, and her hair frizzes. She is not guaranteed to marry a prince.

Does that mean I have to die? Anni asks.

Emmi shrugs. This remains to be seen.

• •

I promise you, you wish you knew my secret.

I promise you, we don't.

It has to do with Charli.

Charlemeanie.

I'll never call her that: she's better than both of you combined.

She's better than you, that's for sure.

Say that louder and one more time to my face!

I'll say whatever I want, and you can't hit me: I'm a girl!

I can't hit you but I can pinch you so hard you'll squeal!

You can't! I'll show the bruises to Papa and he'll strike you!

He won't! He never strikes me! I'm his only son!

He would! He has! I've seen it!

You lie!

He struck you when you bombed Anni's face with your soldiers.

Branni is silent. Emmi is right.

My secret is too good to tell you.

Tell your soldiers, Emmi says. They want amusement.

• •

Betsy-Serena learns of her sister's evil plan because of a loyal courtier named Chestnut. Weeping, she drugs her sister using a tincture of opium, masking the tell-tale odor with cinnamon, and hands her over, still weeping, to the evil Lord Castlering, who mocks her tears. Then, rather than marry Philip, whom she despises for coming between her and her sister, she drinks of the same tincture and lays herself down by the edge of a cliff so she might tumble into it whilst unawares.

Why do sisters always have to die, asks Anni, because she's too young to remember.

The sisters lie in state, reunited in death, young and beautiful in their white dresses, mourned by all who knew them. The sisters always die in Emmi's stories, so new sisters must be born: Mariella, Marietta, Mariposa, and Mariquetta; Libby, Lizzy, Betty, and Eliza. Today, for the first time, they die for a man.

I liked it better when Charli was here, Anni says. When Charli's here the sisters don't have to die.

Emmi slaps her.

She's coming back, Branni shouts. That's the secret! She's coming back! She's staying forever! Then we'll do the stories our way! Ha ha, ho ho!

Branni dances on his top bunk, on his knees, whooping like a Cherokee.

Anni holds her cheek and cries.

Mahmoud Darwish
Translated from Arabic by Fady Joudah

Don't Write History as Poetry

Don't write history as poetry, because the weapon is
The historian. And the historian doesn't get fever
Chills when he names his victims and doesn't listen
To the guitar's rendition. And history is the dailiness
Of weapons prescribed upon our bodies. "The
Intelligent genius is the mighty one." And history
Has no compassion so that we can long for our
Beginning, and no intention so that we can know what's ahead
And what's behind . . . and it has no rest stops by
The railroad tracks for us to bury the dead, for us to look
Toward what time has done to us over there, and what
We've done to time. As if we were of it and outside it.
History is neither logical nor intuitive that we can break
What is left of our myth about happy times,
Nor is it a myth that we can accept our dwelling at the doors
Of judgment day. It is in us and outside us . . . and a mad
Repetition, from the catapult to the nuclear thunder.
Aimlessly we make it and it makes us . . . Perhaps
History wasn't born as we desired, because
The Human Being never existed?
Philosophers and artists passed through there . . .
And the poets wrote down the dailiness of their purple flowers
Then passed through there . . . and the poor believed
In sayings about paradise and waited there . . .
And gods came to rescue nature from our divinity
And passed through there. And history has no
Time for contemplation, history has no mirror
And no bare face. It is unreal reality
Or unfanciful fancy, so don't write it.
Don't write it, don't write it as poetry!

Don DeLillo

Coming Sun. Mon. Tues.

The bitterness and urgency of today's rebellious youth . . . tender and lyrical . . . A social document of aimless teenagers seeking their identity . . . evocative and bittersweet . . . the tragic boomerang of adolescent passions . . . A visual treat . . . somewhat controversial.
 —The *Times*

It is Fifth Avenue in late afternoon in autumn and the shadows darken the street. The boy wears a heavy sweater and desert boots. He has long hair. The girl is pretty. She is wearing a heavy sweater. It is Fifth Avenue or Grosvenor Square. She has lovely eyes. They look in the shop windows. Mannequins in fur and diamonds. Ladies' shoes atop red velvet. An eight million dollar necklace. She whirls and pirouettes, dreaming of inaugural balls or being presented to the Queen. A few middle-aged people stare at her and shake their heads. What is the world coming to. She giggles and takes the boy's hand and they skip away to the park. They walk in the park. Leaves are falling. It is that golden time of day. There are boats on the lake. The sun is going down behind the Dakota Apartments or the London Hilton and she chases a squirrel across the grass in the soft darkening afternoon. Then they are drinking wine. They are in his small room drinking wine. Her eyes are lovely. The boy is talking. He is being bitter about something. Eventually it becomes clear. It's the world. He is being bitter about the world. He chain-smokes and drinks a lot of wine. It is Greenwich Village or the West Side. It is either of those or it is Soho or it is Montmartre. After a while she does a little pirouette and he gets up and stands in front of the bathroom mirror and makes funny faces in the mirror. Then they make funny faces together. He kisses her. She becomes pregnant. She is pregnant and they talk to an abortionist. The abortionist's office is cold and sterile. Everything in the office is white. The boy and girl are nervous but the abortionist's nurse is not nervous. The nurse has hooded eyes.

She smokes a cigarette. The abortionist is smooth and very much to the point. He's been through this scene thousands of times. He has a moustache and long, elegant fingers. He tells them to come back next Tuesday. They leave the office. The boy puts his arm around the girl. They are not on Fifth Avenue. They are near the waterfront. A drunk is sleeping in a doorway. They are trying to decide what to do. The girl writes a letter to her mother in the suburbs and then tears it up. The boy runs from one end of Chicago to the other. Then he looks for a job to get the money for the abortion. He is interviewed by a series of tall men with elegant fingers and they all tell him that they'll let him know if anything turns up. He insults one of the men, an old school chum of his father's who is the president of a management consultant firm and cannot understand why the boy did not finish college. The boy insults him beautifully. The man is so out of it that he is not even sure he has been insulted. Then the boy and girl go to a store in San Francisco or Toronto or Liverpool. They steal some groceries. They leave the store laughing with the groceries under their heavy sweaters. Then the boy stops at a flower stand and steals a flower for the girl. Then they go home and she cries. Then they go to a party. Everybody at the party is a phony except for one guy who's a West Indian or an American Negro or a French Canadian. This guy tells them that they don't know the first thing about being bitter. They have no right to be bitter. He tells them a thing or two about life and death. Everybody else is doing the freddy and this guy is telling them about real suffering, real pain. Telling it like it is. Then he rolls up his sleeve and shows them how he was wounded in Vietnam or Mississippi. Meanwhile everybody is doing the freddy and talking about Andy Warhol or the Animals. The boy and girl go home again. The Vietnam or Mississippi thing has put their troubles in a truer perspective. They play hide-and-seek under the covers of his tiny bed. Then they take turns feeling the girl's belly. They go to the Louvre and the girl sticks out her tongue at the Mona Lisa. Some middle-aged people shake their heads. The next day the girl gets up early and goes to school and the boy sits around smoking and looking in the mirror. Then he steals a car. He drives past all the ancient monuments of Rome or Athens. He sees his father come out of a hotel with a woman who is not his mother. He slumps down low in the driver's seat and watches. His father talks to the woman for a few seconds and then kisses her and they walk off in different directions. The boy just sits there. He sits there. Cars are piling up behind him and horns are blowing. Then he is standing on a bridge above the Thames. Leaves and garbage float by. He goes home and sees that the flower he had stolen for the girl is dead. He throws the flower away so she won't see it when she gets home from school. Then she gets home and tells him to return the stolen car. He gives her a hard time, saying basically that nothing means anything so why bother. She says if that's your concept of life I don't want to see you anymore. So she goes home to the suburbs. She has roast beef and mashed potatoes with her mother and father and older sister. Dessert is chocolate cake. Her mother wants to know why she's failing Civics and Arithmetic and where she's been the last three days and nights. The girl tries to be nice. Things are different now, mom. It's not like when you were growing up. The father makes an attempt at paternal understanding. Takes the positive approach. Compliments her on the fine job she's been doing in English Lit. Says he *likes* the Beatles. Then the older sister's date shows up. He has a crew-cut and wears a button-down shirt. He makes a lot of comments about the junior chamber of commerce and the local country club. He's in the executive training program of a huge management consultant firm. He's also a lieutenant in the Air Force Reserve. Brags about the fact that his country club just admitted its first Jew. The girl wants to know why they didn't do it twenty years ago. Older sister gets mad and tells her to go to her room. In her room she looks in the mirror. Then she feels her belly for a few minutes and repacks her suitcase. The boy stands in front of a movie theater looking at a poster of Jean Paul Belmondo. He goes to a bar. The place is full of hookers and pimps. Derelicts slip from their bar stools and lie in the sawdust. The juke is playing mean, lowdown jazz. The bartender is fat and ugly. A very clean-cut man comes up to the boy and arrests him. The boy's father visits him in jail and they have an argument. The boy doesn't want to mention the strange woman he had seen with his father but in the heat of the argument it slips out. The father is ashamed. He offers to foot all the bills if the boy would only go to the Sorbonne or Michigan State. The boy calls this gesture a moral bribe and he laughs sardonically. Then he is released in the custody of his father and he goes back to his small flat in Chelsea and looks in the mirror. His parole officer tries to talk some sense into him. The parole officer is a nice guy. He has kids of his own, same age as the boy. The boy goes to his room and plays the guitar. He runs through the mad Los Angeles night. Then the girl comes in with her suitcase and they live together. Both of them wear heavy sweaters and blue jeans and desert boots. The girl whirls and pirouettes. She is not too good-looking but she has lovely eyes. They go to Coney Island or Brighton. They ride on the roller coaster and the carousel and they look at themselves in the distorted mirrors. He is nine feet tall and very skinny. She is short and squat and it reminds her that she is pregnant. They think of the abortionist. She feels her belly and smiles. They are going to have the baby. Then he chases her along the beach. Seagulls slant across the dying afternoon. They go behind a sand-dune and kiss. They go home. He kills a roach. They see what their life together is going to be like.

The end.

Brian Doyle

No

The most honest rejection letter I ever received for a piece of writing was from *Oregon Coast Magazine*, to which I had sent a piece that was half bucolic travelogue and half blistering attack on the tendencies of hamlets along the coast to seek the ugliest and most lurid neon signage for their bumper-car emporia, myrtlewood lawn-ornament shops, used-car lots, auto-wrecking concerns, terra-cotta nightmares, and sad moist flyblown restaurants.

"Thanks for your submission," came the handwritten reply from the managing editor. "But if we published it we would be sued by half our advertisers."

This was a straightforward remark and I admire it, partly for its honesty, a rare shout in a world of whispers, and partly because I have, in thirty years as a writer and editor, become a close student of the rejection note. The shape, the color, the prose, the tone, the subtext, the speed or lack thereof with which it arrives, even the typeface or scrawl used to stomp gently on the writer's heart — of these things I sing.

. .

One of the very best: a rejection note sent by the writer Stefan Merken to an editor who had rejected one of his short stories. "Please forgive me for not accepting your rejection letter," wrote Merken. "At this time I cannot accept a rejection of my short story. I accept more than 99 percent of the rejections I receive. Many I don't agree with, but I realize that accepting a piece of fiction for publication is a very subjective judgment call. My acceptance of your rejection letter is also a subjective process and therefore I am returning your letter to you. I did read your letter. I read every letter I receive. Your letter was well-written, but due to time constraints from my own writing schedule, I am unable to make editorial comments. I do make mistakes. Don't you, as an editor, be disheartened by this role reversal. The road of publishing is long and tedious. You need successful publications and I need for successful publications to print my stories. I will expect to see my story in your next publication. Good luck in the future."

• •

The range and scope are astonishing. I have twice received two-page rejection letters from magazines, one an epic and courageous deconstruction of my essay and its many flaws and few virtues, and the other an adventure in sophistry that I still marvel at, in the way you admire a deft bank robber from afar— such astounding creativity, turned to such empty enterprise. In the early days of my own career as an editor I took rejecting pieces very seriously, and tried, as much as possible, to write a thoughtful note explaining why the piece was not quite something for me to accept and pay for. But as all new editors learn, such earnest letters from editors very often are taken by writers as invitations to amend and resubmit pieces, or worse, to argue and debate, and most editors come round eventually to terse generalities simply to defend their working hours and shreds of sanity. Plus I learned that debating poets in particular was painful, although it did give me the chance to daydream about a series of rejection notes designed specifically for poems, which would fault rhythm, meter, cadence, swing, image, line-breaks, verb choice, elusiveness, allusiveness, self-indulgence, self-absorption, liability to lust, and too much muck about love. I nearly had the card printed up that way, with little boxes you could check, like Edmund Wilson's famous EDMUND WILSON REGRETS THAT HE CANNOT . . . , or the lovely form letter that Ursula Le Guin sends to this day, but I got sidetracked by a torrent of devotional poetry that I had to reject posthaste, and never got around to it.

• •

Many magazines lean on a form letter, a printed note, a card, and I study them happily. The *New Yorker*, under the gentle and peculiar William Shawn, sent a gentle yellow slip of paper with the magazine's logo and a couple of gentle sentences saying, gently, no. Under the brisker Robert Gottlieb, the magazine sent a similar note, this one courteously mentioning the "evident quality" of your submission even as the submission is declined. *Harper's* and the *Atlantic* lean on the traditional Thank You But; *Grand Street*, among other sniffy literary quarterlies, icily declines to read your submission if it has not been solicited; the *Sun* responds some months later with a long friendly note from the editor in which he mentions that he is not accepting your piece even as he vigorously commends the writing of it; the *Nation* thanks you for thinking of the *Nation*; and the *Virginia Quarterly Review* sends, or used to send, a lovely engraved card, which is worth the price of rejection. The only rejection notice I keep in plain view is that one, for the clean lines of its limbs and the grace with which it delivers its blow to the groin.

I am no poet, as friends of mine who are poets are quick to remind me, darkly, but here and there I have inflicted poems on various and sundry small quarterlies, and I have come to love the bristle and bustle with which they reject work. I mean, it takes brass balls, as my brothers say, to reject a batch of poems with a curt note while including a *subscription form to the review in the same envelope in which the rejection huddles.* You have to admire the defiant energy there, the passion for persistence. The sheer relentless drive of the small to stay alive is more remarkable, in the end, than the grandeur of the great, no?

• •

Sometimes I daydream of having rejection slips made up for all sorts of things in life, like for moments when I sense a silly argument brewing with my lovely and mysterious spouse, and instead of foolishly trying to lay out my sensible points which have been skewed or miscommunicated, I simply hold up a card (*BRIAN DOYLE REGRETS THAT HE IS UNABLE TO PURSUE THIS MATTER*), or for when my children ask me to drive them half a block to the park (*GET A GRIP*), or when I am invited to a meeting at work I know will drone and moan for hours (*I WOULD PREFER TO HAVE MY SPLEEN REMOVED WITH A BUTTER KNIFE*), or for overpious sermons (*GET A GRIP!*), for oleaginous politicians and other mountebanks (*IF YOU TELL ONE MORE LIE I WILL COME UP THERE AND PUMMEL YOU WITH A MAMMAL*), etc.

On the other hand, what if my lovely and mysterious spouse issued me a rejection slip on the wind-whipped afternoon when I knelt, creaky even then, on a high hill over the wine-dark sea, and stammered *would would would will will will you you marry me*? What if she had leaned down (well, not quite leaned down, she's the size of a heron) and handed me a lovely engraved card that said *WE REGRET TO INFORM YOU THAT WE CANNOT ACCEPT YOUR PROPOSAL, DESPITE ITS*

OBVIOUS MERITS? But she didn't. She did say *yeah*, or I thought she said *yeah*, the wind was really blowing, and then she slapped her forehead and went off on a long monologue about how she couldn't *believe* she said *yeah* when she wanted to say *yes*, her mom had always warned her that if she kept saying *yeah* instead of *yes* there would come a day when she would say *yeah* instead of *yes* and really regret it, and indeed this very day had come to pass, one of those rare moments when your mom was exactly right and prescient, which I often think my mom was when she said to me darkly many years ago *I hope you have kids exactly like you*, the ancient Irish curse. Anyway, there I was on my knees for a while, wondering if my lovely and mysterious paramour had actually said yes, while she railed and wailed into the wind, and finally I said, um, is that an affirmative? because my knees are killing me here, and she said, clearly, yes.

• •

I suppose the whole concept of the editorial Yes is properly the bailiwick of another essay altogether, but I cannot help pondering the positive for a moment, for there are so very many ways to say yes, more than there are to say no, which is interesting on a philosophical and cultural level as well as an editorial one. You can say yes with glee and astonishment, you can say yes with the proviso that you anticipate changing this bit or that, you can say yes while also saying we'll need to sail toward one more draft, you can say yes to a piece of the piece, you can say yes to the idea but not to the piece, or you can, in a sense, say yes to the writer but not to the piece — this isn't quite for us, but we're interested in the verve and bone of your work, call me. The best advice for saying yes I've heard came from a friend of mine who edits a nature magazine. *Use the phone*, he says. *It matters that a voice says yes.* This is the same guy who says you should always envision a writer as your mom when you say no, so as to avoid being snotty, and that you should overpay a young writer on principle once a year, just to mess with the universe.

• •

My friend James and I have for years now plotted a vast essay about editing, an essay we may never write because we have children and paramours and jobs and books to write, but we take great glee in sketching it out, because there are hundreds of subtle joys and crimes of editing, and editing is hardly ever what the non-inky world thinks it is, which is copyediting, which is merely the very last and easiest piece of editing — rather like a crossword puzzle, something you can do near-naked and beer in hand. *Real* editing means staying in touch with lots of writers, and poking them on a fairly regular basis about what they are writing and reading and thinking and obsessing about and what they have always wanted to write but haven't, and also it means sending brief friendly notes to lots of writers you have never worked with yet in hopes that you will, and also it means listening to lots and lots of people about lots and lots of ideas, some or all of which might wend their way into your pages, and it means being hip to the zeitgeist enough to mostly ignore it, and it means reading your brains out, and it means always having your antennae up for what you might excerpt or borrow or steal, and it means tinkering with pieces of writing to make them lean and taut and clear, and always having a small room open in the back of your head where you mix and match pieces to see if they have any zest or magnetism together, and it means developing a third eye for cool paintings and photographs and drawings and sculptures and carvings that might elevate your pages, and writing captions and credits and titles and subheads and contents pages, and negotiating with and calming the publisher, and fawning at the feet of the mailing manager, and wheedling assistants and associates, and paying essayists more than poets on principle, and soliciting letters to the editor, and avoiding conferences and seminars, and sending the printer excellent bottles of wine on every holiday, including Ramadan and Kwanzaa, just in case.

• •

And dickering with photographers, battling in general on behalf of the serial comma, making a stand on behalf of saddle-stitching against the evil tide of perfect-bound publications, halving the number of witticisms in any piece of prose, reading galleys backwards to catch any stupid line breaks or egregious typos, battling on behalf of the semicolon, throwing away all business cards that say PROFESSIONAL WRITER, trying to read over-the-transom submissions within a week of their arrival, deleting the word *unique* on general principle and sending anonymous hate mail to anyone who writes the words *fairly unique*, snarling at writers who write *We must* or *We should* or, God help us all, the word *shan't*, searching with mounting desperation for a scrap or shard or snippet of humor in this bruised and blessed world, reminding male writers that it's OK to acknowledge that there are other people on the planet, halving the number of times any writer says *me* or *I*, checking page numbers maniacally, throwing away cover letters, checking the budget twice a day, and trying to read not most but all of your direct competitors, on the off-chance that there might be something delicious to steal.

And then away to lunch.

• •

My friend James has a lovely phrase for the joy of actually editing a piece: mechanic's delight, he calls it, and I know whereof he speaks, for I have sipped of that cup with a deep and inarticulate pleasure. I have been down in the engine room of very fine writers' minds, my fingers following the snick and slide of their ideas into sentences. I have worked like hercules to clean and repair a flawed piece and bring out the song fenced round by muddle. I have distilled vast wanderings into brief journeys. I have snarled with delight to discover a writer deliberately leaving a fat paragraph for me to cut, a gift he confessed with a grin. I have said no to the great when they were fulsome and yes to the unknown when they were stunning. Many times I have said yes when I should have said no, for all sorts of reasons, some of them good, and more times than I know I said no when I should have said yes.

• •

I have rejected essays but turned them into letters to the editor. I have rejected essays but asked to borrow one or two of their paragraphs for class notes in the back of my magazine. I have rejected essays but recommended submission to another magazine, which is a polite service to the writer, but I have also rejected essays and inflicted the submission on another magazine, which is a venial sin. I have rejected essays by pleading space concerns, which is not always a lie. I have rejected essays I admired for inchoate reasons that can only be caught in the tiny thimble of the word *fit*, about which another essay could be written. *It doesn't quite fit*, could there be any wider and blanker phrase in the language, a phrase that fits all sorts of things?

• •

I was lucky to train under wonderful and testy editors, a long brawling line of them, starting with my dad, who edited a small trade newspaper, laying it out in the basement of our house with redolent rubber cement and long strips of galleys and galley shears the size of your head. He was and is a man of immense dignity and kindness, and no editor or writer ever had a better first editor than my dad, to whom I would show my early awful overwritten overlyrical self-absorbed stories, which he would read slowly and carefully, and then hand them back, saying gently *beginning, middle, end*. I thought he was going nuts early, the old man, but he was telling me, in his gentle way, that my pieces were shallow, and that no amount of lovely prose matters unless it tells a tale—a lesson I have tried to remember daily since.

On my first day as an editor, in Chicago many years ago, beneath the roar and rattle of the elevated train, the first great editor I worked for gave me a gnomic speech about how *we do not use the word hopefully to begin a sentence here*, another remark I never forgot. Later, in Boston, I worked for a very good editor whose mantra was *elevate the reader*, and then I worked, again in Boston, for a genius editor who actually had a bottle of whiskey in his desk and a green eyeshade in his office. He cursed beautifully, in great rushes and torrents, and wrote like a roaring angel, and had been in a rabbinical seminary, and had shoveled shit in an Australian circus, and driven a cab in Brooklyn, and much else. As testy and generous a man as I ever met, and a glorious editor, whose driving theme was *say something real, write true things, cut to the chase*. More advice I have not forgotten (hopefully).

• •

Some of the best yesses I have issued over the years: yes to a sixty-year-old minister in Texas who had never published an essay in his life or even sent one to an editor but he finally wrote down (very slowly, he told me later) a brief piece about the two times in his life, many years apart, a Voice spoke to him out of the air clear as a bell and to his eternal credit he did not in the essay try to explain or comment on these speakings for which refusal to opine I would have kissed him, given the chance. Yes to a twenty-year-old woman who wrote a lean perfect piece about her job running the ancient wooden-horse carousel in a shopping mall. Yes to a sixty-year-old woman who wrote the greatest two-line poem I have ever seen to date. Yes to a thirty-year-old Mormon man who wrote an absolutely haunting essay about laughter (which was also funny). Yes to a twenty-year-old woman who was a waitress in a bar in a rotten part of town and wrote a haunting brief piece about the quiet people who sat at the bar every night when it closed.

Yes to a sixty-year-old man who drives a bus and wrote a piece about a six-year-old girl who was so broken and so hilarious and so brave that when I finished reading the essay I put my face in my hands and wept and wept. Yes to a fifty-year-old doctor who had sent me arch essay after arch essay but finally sent me a perfect essay about the best teacher she ever had, to which I said yes so fast I nearly broke a finger. Yes to half of an essay by Andre Dubus, an essay we were cheerfully arguing about when he died of a heart attack, and I asked his oldest son if I could print the good half and not the mediocre half, and he said yes, which made me smile, for I could almost hear Andre cursing at me happily from the afterworld, in that dark amused growly drawly rumble he had when alive.

. .

When my own essays are rejected I immediately inflict them on another editor, whereas I am always mindful of my dad's advice that a piece isn't really finished unless it is off your desk and onto another's, and I am that lesser species of writer who can never stay focused on One Important Project but always has four or five pieces bubbling at once, so my writing life is a sort of juggling act, with pieces flying here and there, some slumping home through the mailbox and others sailing sprightly away in their Sunday best, eager and open-faced. When one slouches home, weary and dusty, I spruce him up and pop him into the mail and lose track until either he comes home again riddled with arrows or I get a postcard from another desk, sometimes in another country, *I've found a home*!

And then every few years I gather some thirty or forty together again, actually printing them out and spreading them out on the floor, a motley reunion, so as to make a collection of essays, and I have often thought that there is an essay even in this small odd act, their jostling for position, my kneeling over them attentively, worrying again about their health, listening to their changed and seasoned voices, listening for who wants to stand by whom, putting them in parade order like kindergartners bounding off on a field trip, two by two like braces of birds. No one ever talks about the paternal aspect of being a writer, the sending of your children off into the world, where they make their own way, go to work, enter homes, end up in the beds of strangers, and only occasionally do I hear news from the frontier. But such is the wage of age.

..

Why *do* editors say no, anyway? Well, I cannot, of course, speak for All Editors, and I cannot even properly speak for myself, because I reject some pieces from a murky inarticulate intuitive conviction that they're just not our speed, but there are some general truths to note. We say no because we don't print that sort of material. We say no because the topic is too far afield. We say no because we have printed eleven pieces of just that sort in the past year alone. We say no because the writing is poor, muddled, shallow, shrill, incoherent, solipsistic, or insane. We say no because we have once before dealt with the writer and still shiver to remember the agony which we swore to high heaven on stacks of squirrel skulls never to experience again come hell or high water. We say no sometimes because we have said yes too much and there are more than twenty pieces in the hopper and none of them will see the light of day for months and the last of the ones waiting may be in the hopper for more than two years, which will lead to wailing and the gnashing of teeth. We say no because if we published it we would be sued by half our advertisers. We say no because we know full well that this is one of the publisher's two howling bugabears, the other one being restoring American currency to the silver standard. We say no because we are grumpy and have not slept properly and are having dense and complex bladder problems. We say no because our daughters came home yesterday with Mohawk haircuts and boyfriends named Slash. We say no because Britney Spears has sold more records worldwide than Bruce Springsteen. We say no for more reasons than we know.

..

Even now, after nearly thirty years as an editor, years during which I have rejected thousands of essays and articles and poems and profiles and ideas (even once a play, *I have rejected a play*, there's the phrase of the day), I still, even now, often feel a little sadness when I say no. Not always—I feel nothing but cold professionalism when I reject a submission from someone who clearly hasn't the slightest idea or interest in the magazine itself, and is just using the magazine as a generic target for his or her work; for example, people who submit fiction, which we have never published—or never published knowingly, let's say.

But far more often the writers *have* looked at the magazine, and *are* submitting something we might publish, and *did* make it with all their hearts, and it just doesn't make it over the amorphous and inexplicable bar set in my head, and I decline their work with a twinge of regret, for I would so like to say yes, to reward their labor and creativity, the way in which they have opened their hearts and souls, the courage they have shown in bleeding on the page and sending it to a man they do not know, for judgment, for acceptance, for rejection. So very often I find myself admiring grace and effort and craftsmanship, honesty and skill, piercing and penetrating work, even as I turn to my computer to type a rejection note, or reach for one of our own printed rejection slips, to scrawl something encouraging atop my illegible signature. So very many people working so very hard to connect, and here I am, slamming doors day after day.

. .

After lo these many years as a magazine editor I have settled on a single flat sentence for my own use ("Thanks for letting me read your work, but it's not quite right for this magazine," a sentence I have come to love for the vast country of *not quite right*, into which you could cram an awful lot of sins), but I still have enduring affection for the creative no, such as this gem sent to a writer by a Chinese publication: "We have read your manuscript with boundless delight, and if we were to publish your paper, it would be impossible for us to publish any work of a lower standard. And, as it is unthinkable that in the next thousand years we shall see its equal, we are, to our regret, compelled to return your divine composition and beg you a thousand times to overlook our short sight and timidity."

I have been an editor for thirty years, and in those dark and inky years during which my eyesight has gone and my fingertips have been hammered into blunt squares, my patience evaporated and my posture shot to hell, I have never seen, given, or received anything to top that as a rejection notice, and so I conclude as once did that noted editor Henry Louis Mencken, of Baltimore, who once finished a harangue aimed at newspaper editors (whom he called "a gang of pecksniffs") by noting that "no one has asked me for my views, and moreover, my experience in the past has not convinced me that they are desired. So perhaps I had better shut up and sit down," which I do.

Camille T. Dungy

Trophic Cascade

After the reintroduction of gray wolves
to Yellowstone and, as anticipated, their culling
of deer, trees grew beyond the deer stunt
of the midcentury. In their up reach
songbirds nested, who scattered
seed for underbrush, and in that cover
warrened snowshoe hare. Weasel and water shrew
returned, also vole, and so came soon hawk
and falcon, bald eagle, kestrel, and with them
hawk shadow, falcon shadow. Eagle shade
and kestrel shade haunted newly berried
runnels where deer no longer rummaged, cautious
as they were, now, of being surprised by wolves.
Berries brought bear, while undergrowth and willows,
growing now right down to the river, brought beavers,
who dam. Muskrats came to the dams, and tadpoles.
Came, too, the night song of the fathers
of tadpoles. With water striders, the dark
gray American dipper bobbed in fresh pools
of the river, and fish stayed, and the bear, who
fished, also culled deer fawns and to their kill scraps
came vulture and coyote, long gone in the region
until now, and their scat scattered seed, and more
trees, brush, and berries grew up along the river
that had run straight and so flooded but thus dammed,
compelled to meander, is less prone to overrun. Don't
you tell me this is not the same as my story. All this
life born from one hungry animal, this whole,
new landscape, the course of the river changed,
I know this. I reintroduced myself to myself, this time
a mother. After which, nothing was ever the same.

Helen Forman

Ophelia

Forlorn Ophelia draggles everywhere,
An ivory tower for polliwogs,
Her feet and her hands and her shattered hair
Weeping undone as peas and pods.
She was marvelous and tall in her dream.
She was, she was, and she spilled in a stream.

Fallow Ophelia waited, flecked with spring,
Glittering to embrace that prince.
He might salve her mouth, the taut bee sting
Where honey bled. Why did he mince?
He would weave her tapestries of ardor.
She wanted a plain bed founded harder.

The old stream holds forever its cold load,
Lopsided lily sprout of grief.
Never deflowered by the colder toad
Whose soggy thighs clamp to her leaf.
Felon, Ophelia! ruined water buoys
Your green inane careening counterpoise.

Joanna Goodman

Beginning with a Line from NPR

Birds are returning to the city, and not just
pigeons. Last week, on the steps that flame the Met,
we saw a couple: glossed purple epithets
to the morning we'd mustered

together. Obscure wing bars.
They house inside cement — martins,
wide-gaped, thin.
Then through changed air they forge

circles in a glide, like star-
lings shoot straight, without a rise
or fall. A martin flies
direct. Unsure

where to sit, what to say: we
are most ourselves in
silence. The boy, alone, dumb, pretends
nothing in my story. Plucked clean

from human form, wrapped in silk,
he's thrown back
into a clapping
tree: the tree smokes; flick.

The kerchief's done
its trick and he's a bird, put
out to live. Just once I wore a mask to breathe. Sucked
air into the drowned

or almost drowned lace
of our daughter's heart. The beat skimmed clear
across the screen. Am I anywhere
you need? These birds are called escapes.

Linda Gregerson

Cranes on the Seashore

For Thomas Lynch

1.
Today, Tom, I followed the tractor ruts north
        along
            the edge of Damien's pasture. I missed all the

dung slicks but one. The calves did not judge me
        or, comely
           darlings, judged me benign. The ditches

and the token bits of barbed wire weren't, I like
        to think,
           intended to halt my trespass much more than they

did. The hedge-crowned chassis might have been one
        of my father's
           own. And then at the rise, Tom, the promised

North Atlantic, and I'm fixed. Salt cure for
        rheum. Rock
           cure for bureaucracy and blood-borne grudge.

The farmers on Orkney favored this time of year
        for pillage. Took
           to the sea just after the crops were in. Cleared

the mind.

2.
                Megan
      is not happy with her drawing of the

rock face. She has fastened on only this one pure
                thing:
        the light-shot swells of the tide do not move her,

the shattered interlacements and the rolling
                greens,
        she'd trade them all for the one right likeness

of ice-thrust slate. Megan is not by nature
                ascetic — her
        paper has smudged and the pencil lead snapped —

she's after proof the earth leaps too

3.
                At eight
      o'clock on a Wednesday evening, eighteen

hundred seventy-four, one Jeremiah Dowling
                (this
        was June quite near the solstice, therefore

light) took aim "as he thought" at a pair of cranes.
                The girls
        in question, both of them in service at the

Leadmore farm, were washing skeins of new-spun
                wool
        in the surf. And must have bloodied

the wool when they fell, but did not die,
                or had not
        when the county paper went to press.

Of Mr. Dowling's youth and upright family
                the writer
        cannot say enough (his obvious

promise, their moneyed remorse); we may thank
                our different
        pieties we're less inclined to think these

help. We'd like to think our present dis-
                    positions
            bear more scrutiny, that girls

may be lovely as cranes and safe.

4.
                    Behind
            the row of holiday villas, the hay

has started to rot in the fields. On the weather,
                    the hay
            and the holiday makers agree. But Damien's

calves have all been sound, and three to
                    come,
            and Damien's father is glad for the extra (villas

need carpenters) work. It's like this at home now, the parts
                    you sell in order
            to pay for the parts you keep, till my uncle

is told by the barman one day would he please
                    not come in
            in his farm clothes, it puts off trade. A little

longer, barman, bid the locals then, A little
                    while
            is all we'll take. I lied

about the calves, though; you can see the smallest
                    Holstein's
            lame. Emma had thought he was simply less

greedy, so late did he turn toward the bucket of mash,
                    and now
            she can hardly bear to look. God

keep us from the gun sight. Here is
                    one
            for the landlord and one (we're almost

gone) for the road.

Kimiko Hahn

Circles and Breasts

"A fertility signal, a youth signal, a health signal, a wealth symbol."
A gland and a store of fat.

"Mama" or, "¡Oye mamita!" if looking for a steamy date.
Preferably with real tissue.

For myself, though born in the Fifties: pillow and/or punishment.
For myself, against the cliché of gravity

as I strip down for the unstoppable mirror.
For the Amazon, cutting off the right side

in order to shoot her arrow
                            straight into the adversary.

Note
    Quoted portions are from Natalie Angier's article "The Circular Logic of the Universe," *New York Times*, December 8, 2009.

Githa Hariharan

Diablo Baby

Which one of you is my father?

I know what you, with the twitching lips, and you, and you — with the knotting eyebrows and bulging notebook — will say. The obvious thing. Ask your mother.

I have. She speaks to me (and sings to me and dances for me) just as a mother should. And I, Diablo Baby, talk to her. I never gooed and gaaed and gurgled like other mothers' babies. Why pretend to be ordinary when you are not?

But when I ask her the big question, all she can do is show me a tattered rag of a sari. It is bleached cotton, so old, frayed and grimy that it could be a strip of dry bark curling at the edges. But the picture on it glistens; white chalk flesh, yellow and red hibiscus of vegetable dye. There is a body in the picture, a body that has trapped the glint of silver in its bulges and ripples and folds. A piece of bloated moon that sits on a carpet of succulent forest flowers, on a sheet of smooth, fiery blood.

I have looked at this image many times. In it my reflection holds still. (When I look at myself in the stream, the water trembles, afraid of my steady gaze, my horns, my tattoos.)

My mother made the picture. She also made me. She thinks she had some help there, though she knows no names to name. When I ask her, Where is my father, she replies, In my head.

Then you came, she says, so we don't need him any more. And we have the picture, don't we? And the story in the picture?

So if I want a father, I must mine a story as strange and raggedy as my mother. A story with a forest girl, a temple, a church, a baby. And a blue-white, horned, phantom lover.

On the edge of the forest was a village and in the heart of the village were two buildings, one on the right side of the dusty street, one on the left. The buildings could have been brothers, so alike were their mortared, whitewashed walls. But like many brothers, their heads were somewhat different. The building to the right, a temple, had a brick pyramid for a head. A tapering triangle of a *gopuram* sat like a stiff hat pulled down over its face. At the tip of this hat, a solitary red flag waved in the breeze. A piece of the flag was cut out of its right side so that what remained was a trembling, open mouth.

The building to the left, a church, had a more modest, flat head. But a huge bell filled up the balcony that jutted out of its forehead. Even bigger and more impressive was the cross crowning the roof. The cross was painted a dazzling white that sucked in the sunlight and threw a halo around itself.

Every morning at daybreak, a girl in a torn, dirty sari carrying a basket and a broom made her way to the temple. As usual there was a big brass tray waiting for her on the step nearest the open front door. She put down her broom and uncovered the basket that was covered with a piece of damp cloth. She emptied the basketful of blazing red and pink and orange hibiscus onto the brass plate. Then she picked up the broom and went around to the backyard where yesterday's flowers lay in a limp and fleshy pile along with everything else that had been swept out of the temple. She filled the basket with this rubbish, sorting it first to see what was there. Anything edible she pulled out and slipped into the little bundle tied to the end of her sari.

The temple-priest called out to her as he did every morning. Hey Sukhi, he said. The flowers are really fresh this morning. I don't know where you manage to find them. Do you want some pieces of coconut?

Sukhi nodded and he threw a large handful in her direction. She picked up the pieces and sat on her haunches, chewing.

He lingered at the back door while she ate. He was bald, with a tuft of hair at the back of his head. He was always bare-chested, and the jungle of dark hair on his chest made him look like a tame bear.

He frowned at the broom lying by her.

Still working for the foreign devil? he asked. Why do you go to the white man's temple?

Sukhi stopped chewing and considered this with puzzlement. Who is a devil? she asked. And why is he white?

He sniggered and threw her a few more pieces of coconut. You'll find out soon enough, he said, looking at her knowingly. You keep sweeping that church day after day and you'll meet the devil all right. A white devil with a blazing cross on his heart. Gray eyes shining out of his chalk face like a hungry cat.

Sukhi picked up her broom and basket. You stop working there if you know what's good for you, he called after her.

Sukhi swept the church with her broom; her basket was now filled to the brim with junk from both temple and church. Then she dusted and polished the silver cup at the altar.

The church-priest gave her a coin. He also gave her something to eat. She liked sitting in the church's backyard, chewing and thinking her own thoughts. But neither the temple-priest nor the church-priest could leave her alone. Neither could do without her, so lovely and fresh were the flowers she brought every morning, and so well did she sweep and dust and polish.

Now the church-priest began his usual sermon as she ate. Still taking flowers to that temple? he asked, eyeing the wilted flowers in her basket.

My child, he said, his voice growing rich and sonorous. Come home to this church and be saved. Remember what I have told you. The devil is always watching you from where he sits burning in hell. He waits, the devious snake, to open his mouth and strike. He is horned; he is lecherous. When he sees the bare breasts under your sari, when he finds your untouched soul, do you think he will let you go?

Ah, the devil again, thought Sukhi, and she listened carefully. Though the temple-priest and the church-priest can't bear each other, they have this mysterious devil in common.

Her head was full of the devil as she made her way back into the forest. The forest was still, in a deep, stupefied sleep. In fact, the forest that afternoon was a fit place for the devil, if he really liked fire as much as the priests said he did. She could feel the relentless fire on her head and back and feet as she made her way, a single thought throbbing in her head, never pausing till she reached the pool. The watering hole was deserted except for a few thirsty birds that took wing as she neared the water.

She was hot, so hot. She pulled the filthy sari off her body and went naked into the water. The world outside her closed eyes was a furious blur of orange.

She thought she felt something cool slither up her leg. It could have been a water snake, but she did not move. Instead she heard herself whispering playfully, teasingly, Devil, are you here? Are you watching me?

She floated. She must have floated for hours, or floated into sleep, or into a dream. In this place where she had drifted, a lost and empty boat looking for its moorings, the fiery world waiting outside her eyelids had vanished. The heat had dissolved, so had the priests, and her hungry sunburnt body in the muddy forest pool. The cool-tongued intruder making his way up her leg lived in this place where there was no thirst, no drudge of filling the belly. The fire on her skin was being put out. The anger and bewilderment in her heart were dying. And at the very last moment, just before the coolness slipped out of her and left her, she saw, though her eyes were still shut, an image she could capture again in meticulous, three-dimensional detail. She need never be alone again. She saw a baby plump with her desire, sharp-horned, self-possessed. On his body he flaunted all the caste marks of his paternity, or the lack of it.

Bob Hicok

How Origami Was Invented

The last I went to confession was to whisper
I like being alone. I was penanced to sing
"Stayin' Alive" one hundred times. Solitude
almost tastes like grapes, of course not
but alone I can think such things,
there's no one to counter *strawberries*.
Particularly the Big Holidays are a good time
to have a conversation with buildings,
everyone's gone, to talk with buildings
you merely lean against them,
they do the rest, brick is thrilled
to be touched, marble, I shun marble, so
haughty. Cities need to be alone and oceans
and the moon gets too much credit
let's leave it out of this. I've been given
vast sympathy for this affliction.
Did you know the face of someone who thinks
you're a loser
slash
psychotic looks like a photo of Nixon
lifted from newspaper with Silly Putty
and stretched? While thinking of that sentence
remember this isn't a science.
If I was not alone sometimes I'd all the time
not want to be with people. This
because we invented Spandex and chit chat.
Other species invent beehives and asexual
reproduction and spots on wings that look
like eyes but are just spots.
Sometime I wish the mouth

looked like the mouth but was just the mouth
being kissed. The mouth
kissed both presents and works against
solitude. If that idea were origami
I'd refold it into a heron. I can't, not yet,
but I'm alone this weekend and there's paper
everywhere on which I've tried
to write a clear path to you.

Alice Hoffman

The Witch of Truro

1801

Witches take their names from places, for places are what give them their strength. The place need not be beautiful, or habitable, or even green. Sand and salt, so much the better. Scrub pine, plumberry and brambles, better still. From every bitter thing, after all, something hardy will surely grow. From every difficulty, the seed that's sown is that much stronger. Ruin is the milk all witches must drink; it's the lesson they learn and the diet they're fed upon. Ruth Declan lived on a bluff that was called Blackbird's Hill, and so she was called Ruth Blackbird Hill, a fitting name, as her hair was black and she was so light-footed she could disappear right past a man and he wouldn't see anything, he'd just feel a rush of wind and pick up the scent of something reminiscent of orchards and the faint green odor of milk.

Ruth kept cows, half a dozen, but they gave so much into their buckets she might have had twenty. She took her cows for walks, as though they were pets, along the sand-rutted King's Highway, down to the bay where they grazed on marsh grass. Ruth Blackbird Hill called her cows her babies and hugged them to her breast; she patted their heads and fed them sugar from the palm of her hand, and that may have been why their milk was so sweet. People said Ruth Blackbird Hill sang to her cows at night, and that whoever bought milk from her would surely be bewitched. Not that anyone believed in such things anymore. All the same, when Ruth came into town, the old women tied bits of hemp into witchknots on their sleeves for protection. The old men looked to see if she was wearing red shoes, always the mark of a witch. Ruth avoided these people; she didn't care what they thought. She would have happily stayed on Blackbird Hill and never come down, but two things happened: first came smallpox, which took her father and her mother, no matter how much sassafras tea they were given, and how tenderly Ruth cared for them. Then came the fire, which took the house and the land.

On the night of the fire, Ruth Blackbird Hill stood in the grass and screamed. People could hear her in Wellfleet and in Eastham and far out to sea. She watched the pear and the apple and the peach trees burning. She watched the grass turn red as blood. She had risked her life to save her cows, running into the smoky barn, and now they gathered round her, lowing, leaking milk, panicked. It was not enough that she should lose her mother and her father, one after another, now she had lost Blackbird Hill, and with it she had lost herself. The fire raged for two days until a heavy rain began to fall. People in town said that Ruth killed a toad and nailed it to a hickory tree, knowing that rain would follow, but it was too late. The hill was burned to cinders; it was indeed a blackbird's hill, black as night, black as the look in Ruth's eyes, black as the future that was assuredly hers.

Ruth sat on the hillside until her hair was completely knotted and her skin was the color of the gray sky up above. She might have stayed there forever, but after some time went by, her cows began to cry. They were weak with hunger, they were her babies still, and so Ruth took them into town. One day, people looked out their windows and a blackbird seemed to swoop by, followed by a herd of skinny milk-cows that had all turned to pitch in the fire. Ruth Blackbird Hill made herself a camp right on the beach; she slept there with no shelter, no matter the weather. The only food she ate was what she dug up in the shallows: clams and whelks. She may have drunk the green, thin milk her cows gave, though it was still tinged with cinders. She may have bewitched herself to protect herself from any more pain. Perhaps that was the reason she could sleep in the heat or the rain; why it was said she could drink salt water.

Anyone would have guessed the six cows would have bolted for someone else's farmland and a field of green grass, but they stayed where they were, on the beach, beside Ruth. People in town said you could hear them crying at night; it got so bad the fish were frightened out of the bay, and the whelks disappeared, and the oysters buried themselves so deeply they couldn't be found.

It was May, the time of year when the men were at sea. Perhaps there might have been a different decision made if the men had been home from the Great Banks and the Middle Banks, where their sights were set on mackerel and cod. Perhaps Ruth would have been run out of town. As it was, Susan Crosby and Easter West devised a plan of their own. They won Ruth Blackbird Hill over slowly, with plates of oatcakes and kettles of tea. They took their time, the way they might have with a fox or a dove, any creature that might be easily startled. They sat on a log of driftwood and told Ruth that sorrow was what this world was made of, but that it was her world still. At first she would not look at them, yet they could tell she was listening. She was a young woman, a girl really, nineteen at most, although her hands looked as hard as an old woman's, with ropes of veins that announced her hardships.

Susan and Easter brought Ruth over to Lysander Wynn's farm, where he'd built a blacksmithing shed. It took half the morning to walk there, with the cows stopping to graze by the road, dawdling until Ruth coaxed them on. It was a bright blue day and the women from town felt giddy now that they'd made a firm decision to guide someone else's fate, what their husbands might call interference had they but known. As for Ruth, she still had a line of black cinders under her fingernails. There was eelgrass threaded through her hair. She had the notion that these two women, Susan and Easter, known for their good works and their kindly attitudes, were about to sell her. She simply couldn't see any other reason for them to be walking along with her, swatting the cows on the rear to speed them on, waving away the flies. The awful thing was that Ruth wasn't completely opposed to being sold. She didn't want to think. She didn't want to ask questions. She didn't even want to speak.

They reached the farm that Lysander had bought from the Hadley family. He'd purchased the property mainly because it was the one place in the area from which there was no view of the sea, for that was exactly what he wanted. The farm was only a mile from the closest shore, but it sat in a hollow, with tall oaks and scrub pine and a field of sweet peas and brambles nearby. As a younger man, Lysander had been a sailor, he'd gone out with the neighbors to the Great Banks, and it was there he'd had his accident. A storm had come up suddenly, and the sloop had tilted madly, throwing Lysander into the sea. It was so cold he had no time to think, save for a fleeting thought of Jonah, of how a man could be saved when he least expected it, in ways he could have never imagined.

He wondered if perhaps the other men on board, Joseph Hansen and Edward West, had had the foresight to throw him a side of salt pork for him to lean on, for just when he expected to drown, something solid was suddenly beneath him. Something hard and cold as ice. Something made of scales rather than flesh or water or wood; a creature who certainly was not intent on Lysander's salvation. The fish to whose back he clung was a halibut, a huge one, two hundred, maybe three hundred pounds, Edward West later said. Lysander rode the halibut like he rode his horse, Domino, until he was bucked off. All at once his strength was renewed by his panic; he started swimming, harder than he ever had before. Lysander was almost to the boat when he felt it, the slash of the thing against him, and the water turned red right away. He was only twenty at the time, too young to have this happen. Dead or alive, either would have been better than what had befallen him. He wished he had drowned that day, because when he was hauled into the boat, they had to finish the job and cut off the leg at the thigh, then cauterize the wound with gunpowder and whiskey.

Lysander had some money saved, and the other men in town contributed the rest, and the farm was bought soon after. The shed was built in a single afternoon, and the anvil brought down from Boston. Luckily, Lysander had the blacksmith's trade in his family, on his father's side, so it came naturally to him. The hotter the work was, the better he liked it. He could stick his hand into the flame fueled by the bellow and not feel a thing. But let it rain, even a fleeting drizzle, and he would start to shiver. He ignored the pond behind the house entirely, though there were catfish there that were said to be delectable. Fishing was for other men. Water was for fools. As for women, they were a dream he didn't bother with. In his estimation, the future was no farther away than the darkness of evening; it consisted of nothing more than a sprinkling of stars in the sky.

Lysander used a crutch made of applewood that bent when he leaned upon it, but was surprisingly strong when the need arose. He had hit a prowling skunk on the head with the crutch and knocked it unconscious. He had dug through a mat of moss for a wild orchid that smelled like fire when he held it up to his face. He slept with the crutch by his side in bed, afraid to be without it. He liked to walk in the woods, and sometimes he imagined he would be better off if he just lay down between the logs and the moss and stayed there, forevermore. Then someone would need their horse shod; they'd come up the road and ring the bell hung on the wall of the shed, and Lysander would have to scramble back from the woods. But he thought about remaining where he was, hidden, unmoving; he imagined it more often than anyone might have guessed. Blackbirds would light upon his shoulders, crickets would crawl into his pockets, fox would lie down beside him and never even notice he was there.

He was in the woods on the day they brought Ruth Blackbird Hill and her cows to the farm. Sometimes when he was very quiet Lysander thought he saw another man in the trees. He thought it might be the sailor who'd built the house, the widow Hadley's husband, who'd been lost at sea. Or perhaps it was himself, weaving in and out of the shadows, the man he might have been.

Susan Crosby and Easter West explained the situation, the parents lost, the house and meadows burned down, the way Ruth was living on the beach, unprotected, unable to support herself, even to eat. In exchange for living in Lysander's house, she would cook and clean for him. Ruth kept her back to them as they discussed her fate; she patted one of her cows, a favorite of hers she called Missy. Lysander Wynn was just as bitter as Ruth Blackbird Hill was. He was certain the women from town wouldn't have brought Ruth to the farm if he'd been a whole man, if he'd been able to get up the stairs to the attic where they suggested Ruth sleep. He was about to say no, he was more than willing to get back to work in the fires of his shop, when he noticed that Ruth was wearing red boots. They were made of old leather, mud-caked, but all the same, Lysander had never seen shoes that color, and he felt touched in some way. He thought about the color of fire. He thought about flames. He thought he would never be hot enough to get the chill out of his body or the water out of his soul.

"Just as long as she never cooks fish," he heard himself say.

Ruth Blackbird Hill laughed at that. "What makes you think I cook at all?"

Ruth took the cows into the field of sweet peas. Lysander's horse, Domino, rolled his eyes and ran to the far end of the meadow, spooked. But the cows paid no attention to him whatsoever, they just huddled around Ruth Blackbird Hill and calmly began to eat wild weeds and grass. What Lysander had agreed to didn't sink in until Susan Crosby and Easter West left to go back to town. "Hasn't this woman any belongings?" Lysander had called after them. "Not a thing," they replied. "The cows that follow her and the shoes on her feet."

Well, a shoe was the one thing Lysander might have offered. He had several old boots thrown into a cabinet, useless when it came to his missing right foot. He put out some old clothes and some quilts at the foot of the stairs leading to the attic. He'd meant to finish the attic, turn the space into decent rooms, but he'd had to crawl up the twisting staircase to check on the rafters, and that was enough humiliation to last him for a very long time. Anyway, the space was good enough for someone used to sleeping on the beach. When Ruth didn't come in to start supper, Lysander made himself some johnnycake, half-cooked, but decent enough, along with a plate of turnips; he left half of what he'd fixed on the stair as well, though he had his suspicions that Ruth might not eat. She might just starve herself sitting out in that field. She might take flight and he'd find nothing when he woke, except for the lonely cows mooing sorrowfully.

As it turned out, Ruth was there in the morning. She'd eaten the food he'd left out for her and was already milking the cows when Lysander went out to work on a metal harness for Easter West's uncle, Karl. Those red shoes peeked out from beneath Ruth's black skirt. She was singing to the cows and they were waiting in line, patiently. The horse, Domino, had come closer and Ruth Blackbird Hill opened her palm and gave him a lick of sugar.

In the afternoon Lysander saw her looking in the window of the shed. The fire was hot and he was sweating. He wanted to sweat out every bit of cold ocean water. He always built the fire hotter than advisable. He needed it that way. Sometimes he got a stomachache, and when he vomited, he spit out the halibut's teeth. Those teeth had gone right through him, it seemed. He could feel them, cold, silvery things.

He must have looked frightening as he forged the metal harness, covered with soot, hot as the devil, because Ruth Blackbird Hill ran away, and she didn't come to fetch the dinner he placed on the stair — though the food was better than the night before, cornbread with wild onions this time, and greens poured over with gravy. All the same, the following morning, the plate was clean and resting on the table. Every morsel had been eaten.

Ruth Blackbird Hill didn't cook and she didn't clean, but she kept on watching him through the window that was made out of bumpy glass. Lysander didn't look up, didn't let on that he knew she was staring, and then one day she was standing in the doorway to the shed. She was wearing a pair of his old britches and a white shirt, but he could see through the smoke that she had on those red shoes.

"How did you lose your leg?" Ruth asked.

He had expected nearly anything but that question. It was rude; no one asked things like that.

"A fish bit it off," he said.

Ruth laughed and said, "No."

He could feel the heat from the iron he was working on in his hands, his arms, his head.

"You don't believe me?" He showed her the chain he wore around his neck, strung with halibut teeth. "I coughed these up one by one."

"No," Ruth said again, but her voice was quieter, like she was thinking it over. She walked right up to him and he felt something inside him quicken. He had absolutely no idea of what she might do.

Ruth Blackbird Hill put her left hand in the fire, and she would have kept it there if he hadn't grabbed her arm and pulled her back.

"See?" she said to him. Her skin felt cool and she smelled like grass. "There are things I'm afraid of, too."

People in town forgot about Ruth; they didn't think about how she was living out at the farm any more than they remembered how she'd been camped on the beach for weeks without anyone offering her help until Susan and Easter could no longer tolerate her situation. Those two women probably should have minded their own business as well, but they were too kindhearted for that, and too smart to ever tell their husbands what part they had played in Ruth Blackbird Hill living at Lysander's farm. In truth, they had nearly forgotten about her themselves. Then one day Easter West found a pail of milk at her back door. As it turned out Susan Crosby discovered the very same thing on her porch — cool, green milk that tasted so sweet, so very filling, that after a single cup a person wouldn't want another drop to drink all day. Susan chose to go about her business, but Easter was a more curious individual. One night, Easter had dreamed of blackbirds, and of her husband, who was out in the Middle Banks fishing for mackerel. When she woke she had a terrible thirst for fresh milk. She went out to the farm that day, just to have a look around.

There was Ruth in the field, riding that old horse Domino, teaching him to jump over a barrel while the cows gazed on, disinterested. When she saw Easter, Ruth left the horse and came to meet her at the gate. That past night, Ruth herself had dreamed of tea, and of needles and thread set to work, and of a woman who was raising three sons alone while her husband was off to sea. She had been expecting Easter, and had a pail of milk waiting under the shade of an oak tree. The milk was greener than ever, and sweeter than ever too; Easter West drank two tin cupfuls before she realized that Ruth Blackbird Hill was crying.

It was near the end of summer. Everything was blooming and fresh, but it wouldn't last long.

"What is it?" Easter said. "Does he make you work too hard? Is he cruel?"

Ruth shook her head. "It's just that I'll never get what I want. It's not possible."

"What is it you want?"

There was the scent of cows, and of hay, and of smoke from the blacksmith's shop. Ruth had been swimming in the pond behind the house earlier in the day and her hair was shiny; she smelled like water and her skin was cool even in the heat of the day.

"It doesn't matter. Whenever I want something, I don't get it. No matter what it might be. That's the story of my life."

When Easter was leaving, Lysander Wynn came out of his shop. He was leaning on his crutch. He wanted something, too. He wasn't yet thirty, and his work made him strong in his arms and his back, but he felt weak deep inside, bitten by something painful and sharp.

"What did she tell you?" he asked Easter West.

"She's afraid she won't get what she wants," Easter said.

Lysander thought this over while he finished up working. He thought about it while he made supper, a corn and tomato stew. When he left Ruth's dinner on the stair he left a note as well. *I'll get you anything you want.*

That night, Lysander dreamed he wouldn't be able to give Ruth what she asked for, despite his promise. She would want gold, of which he had none. She would want to live in London, on the other side of the ocean. She would want another man, one with two legs who didn't spit out halibut teeth, who didn't fear rain and pondwater. But in the morning, he found a note by the anvil in his shed. What she seemed to want was entirely different from anything he had imagined. *Bring me a tree that has pears the color of blood. The same exact color as my shoes.*

The next day, Lysander Wynn hitched up his horse to a wagon and left on the King's Highway. He went early, while the cows were still sleeping in the field, while the blackbirds were quiet and the fox were still running across the sandy ruts in the road. Ruth knew he was gone when she woke because there was no smoke spiraling from the chimney in the shed; when Edward Hastings came to get his horse shod, no one answered his call. Ruth Blackbird Hill took care of the cows, then she went into the shed herself. She put her hand into the ashes — they were still hot, embers continuing to burn from the day before. She thought about red grass and burning trees and her parents calling out for her to save them. She kept her hand there, unmoving, until she couldn't stand the pain anymore.

He was gone for two weeks, and he never said exactly where he'd been. He admitted only that he'd been through Providence and on into Connecticut. What he didn't say was that he would have gone farther still if it had been necessary. He had no time frame in mind of when he might return. He would have kept on even if snow had begun to fall, if the orchards had turned so white it would have been impossible to tell an apple tree from a plum, a grapevine from a trellis of wisteria.

Lysander planted the pear tree right in front of the house. While he was working, Ruth brought him a cold glass of milk that made him feel like weeping. She showed him her burned hand, then she took off her shoes and stood barefoot in the grass. He hoped what he'd been told in Connecticut was true. The last farmer he'd gone to was experienced with fruit trees, and his orchard was legendary. When Lysander had wanted a guarantee, the old farmer had told him that often what you grew turned out to be what you had wanted all along. He said there was a fine line between crimson and scarlet, and that a person simply had to wait to see what appeared. Ruth wouldn't know until the following fall whether or not the pears would be red, nearly a full year, but she was hopeful that by that time, she wouldn't care.

Randall Jarrell

The Winter's Tale

The storm rehearses through the bewildered fields
Its general logic; the contorted or dispassionate
Faces work out their incredulity, or stammer
The mistaking sentences. Night falls. In the lit
Schoolroom the hothouse guests are crammed
With their elaborate ignorance, repeat
The glib and estranged responses of the dead
To the professor's nod. The urgent galleries
Converge in anticipation on the halls
Where at announced hours the beauty,
Able, and Laughable commence patiently
The permanent recital of their aptitudes:
The song of the world. To the wicked and furred,
The naked and curious, the instruments proffer
Their partial and excessive knowledge; here in the suites,
Among the grains, the contraceptives and textiles,
Or inside the board cave lined with newspapers
Where in one thoroughly used room are initiated,
Persevered in, and annihilated, the forbidding ranges
Of the bewildered and extravagant responses of the cell;
Among all the inexhaustible variations — of milieu,
Of compensation and excess — the waltz-theme shudders,
Frivolous, inexorable, the inadequate and conclusive
Sentence of our genius.
Along the advertisements the blisses flicker,
Partial as morphine, the terminal moraine
Of sheeted continents, a calendar of woe.

We who have possessed the world
As efficiently as a new virus; who classified the races,

Species, and cultures of the world as scrub
To be cleared, stupidity to be liquidated, matter
To be assimilated into the system of our destruction;
Are finding how quickly the resistance of our hosts
Is built up — can think, "Tomorrow we may be remembered
As a technologist's nightmare, the megalomaniacs
Who presented to posterity as their justification
The best armies that the world ever saw."
Who made virtue and poetry and understanding
The prohibited reserves of the expert, of workers
Specialized as the ant-soldier; and who turned from their difficult
Versions to the degenerate myth, the cruelties
So incredible and habitual they seemed escapes.

Yet, through our night, just as before,
The discharged thief stumbles, nevertheless
Weeps at its crystals, feels at the winter's
Tale the familiar and powerful delight;
The child owns the snow-man; the skier
Hesitant along the stormy crest, or wrenching
His turn from the bluff's crust, to glide
Down the stony hillside past the robbers' hut
To the house of the typhoid-carrier; the understanding
Imperturbable in their neglect, concentrating
In obscure lodgings the impatient genius
That informs all the breasts; the few who keep
By lack or obstinacy scraps of the romantic
And immediately adequate world of the past — the
Strangers with a stranger's inflections, the broken
And unlovely English of the unborn world:

All, all, this winter night
Are weak, are emptying fast. Tomorrow puffs
From its iron centers into the moonlight, men move masked
Through streets abrupt with excavations, the explosive triumphs
Of a new architecture: the twelve-floor dumps
Of smashed stone starred with limbs, the monumental
Tombs of a whole age. A whole economy;
The fiascoes of the metaphysician, a theology's disasters,
The substitutes of the geometer for existence, the observation
Of peas and galaxies — the impatient fictions

Of the interminable and euphuist's metaphor exploding
Into use, into breath, into terror; the millennia
Of patience, of skills, of understanding, the centuries
Of terms crystallizing into weapons, the privative
And endless means, the catastrophic
Magnificence of paranoia; are elaborated into
A few bodies in the torn-up street.
The survivor poking in the ruins with a stick
Finds only portions of his friends. In this universe
Of discourse the shameless and witless facility
Of such a conclusion is normal, and no one thinks:
"What came before this was worse. Expected so long,
Arrived at last, tomorrow is death."

From the disintegrating bomber, the mercenary
Who has sown without hatred or understanding
The shells of the absolute world that flowers
In the confused air of the dying city
Plunges for his instant of incandescence, acquiesces
In our death and his own, and welcomes
The fall of the western hegemonies.

Allison Joseph

Barbie's Little Sister

How terrible it would be
to be Barbie's little sister,
suspended in perpetual pre-adolescence
while Barbie, hair flying behind her
in a tousled blond mane, dashed
from adventure to adventure,
ready for space travel or calf roping
or roller disco in campy, flashy clothes
that defied good taste and reason.
Stuck with the awful nickname Skipper,
Barbie's little sis never got out much,
a mere boarder in Barbie's three-story
hot-pink Dream House, too young
to wear the thousands of outfits
stashed in the bedroom closets:
purple-beaded Armani evening gowns,
knit sweater dresses by Donna Karan,
specially commissioned tennis togs
sewn personally by Oleg Cassini.
Skipper had to buy off the rack
at Kmart, condemned to wear
floral sunsuits with Peter Pan collars.
Unlike her bosomy sister,
Skipper had no chest
for the boys to ogle,
until some bright toymaker
gave us "Growing Up Skipper":
with a twist of her right arm,
she grew taller, breasts sprouting
where there once were none,

a thick rubber band inside her
pushing her chest up and out
until the band snapped
and Skipper was stuck at age 15,
never the same again.
For consolation, she turned to
Barbie's black friend Christie —
who was just figuring out
all the fuss about equal rights —
and Barbie's best pal Midge,
who was tired of hearing
about spats with Ken, knowing
he was cheating on America's sweetheart
with every new celebrity doll on the market —
Brooke Shields, Cher, Dorothy Hamill.
Together, those three decided
they'd had enough of Toyland —
so they pooled their cash,
swiped Barbie's camper,
and tore out of California
for Las Vegas, where they bought
a little establishment not too far
from the gaming houses,
a restaurant for all of us
without thick manes of hair
or upturned noses, without
impossibly slender ankles
and tiny feet, without
perfectly molded breasts.

Fady Joudah

Ladies and Gentlemen

… the easiest pain is someone else's,
And even the Hittites

Kept their nuclear weapon a sole possession
For as long as they could.

But it's been a bit much to take since then,
One exodus after another,
Like getting used to the life of

Frequent flyer miles
Without ever cashing them in.

Ladies & gentlemen,
Life will get old soon
And death has long been part of the treatment plan.

What's the use of a flag
Without a land that believes
In poetry and no more

Contused waters to cross?
It's nothing special this waiting
For what will never be

One's own twice.
A flesh wound merely,
An eggplant bruise of a myth.

Ladies & gentlemen, my friends
Of the jury, if you were born in Tokyo

Would you be Japanese?
Or Athens, Georgia, or Rome, Ohio,
Or the land of cactus wind

Where the one-eyed are many: *Why
Do they call the Black Sea, black?*

Because it's always mourning the Dead one.
What doesn't evaporate burns.

Konstantinos Kavaphes
Translated from Greek by Richmond Lattimore

Waiting for the Barbarians

Why are we all assembled and waiting in the market place?

It is the barbarians; they will be here today.

Why is there nothing being done in the senate house?
Why are the senators in session but are not passing laws?

Because the barbarians are coming today.
Why should the senators make laws any more?
The barbarians will make the laws when they get here.

Why has our emperor got up so early
and sits there at the biggest gate of the city
high on his throne, in state, and with his crown on?

Because the barbarians are coming today
and the emperor is waiting to receive them
and their general. And he has even made ready
a parchment to present them, and thereon
he has written many names and many titles.

Why have our two consuls and our praetors
come out today in their red embroidered togas?
Why have they put on their bracelets with all those amethysts
and rings shining with the glitter of emeralds?
Why will they carry their precious staves today
which are decorated with figures of gold and silver?

Because the barbarians are coming today
and things like that impress the barbarians.

Why do our good orators not put in any appearance
and make public speeches, and do what they generally do?

Because the barbarians are coming today
and they get bored with eloquent public speeches.

Why is everybody beginning to be so uneasy?
Why so disordered? (See how grave all the faces have
become!) Why do the streets and the squares empty so quickly,
and they are all anxiously going home to their houses?

Because it is night, and the barbarians have not got here,
and some people have come in from the frontier
and say that there aren't any more barbarians.

What are we going to do now without the barbarians?
In a way, those people were a solution.

Brigit Pegeen Kelly

Dead Doe: I

for Huck

The doe lay dead on her back in a field of asters: no.

The doe lay dead on her back beside the school bus stop: yes.

Where we waited.
Her belly white as a cut pear. Where we waited: no: off

from where we waited: yes:

at a distance: making a distance
we kept,
as we kept her dead run in sight, that we might see if she chose
to go skyward;
that we might run, too, turn tail
if she came near
and troubled our fear with presence: with ghostly blossoming: with the
   fountain's
                                           unstoppable blossoming
                   and the black stain the algae makes when the water
                                                stays near.
We can take the gilt-edged strolling of the clouds: yes.
But the risen from the dead: no!

The haloey trouble shooting of the goldfinches in the bush:
                     yes: but *in season*:

kept within bounds,
not in the pirated rows of corn,
not above winter's pittance of river.

The doe lay dead: she lent
    her deadness to the morning, that the morning might have weight, that
        our waiting might matter: be upheld by significance: by light
        on the rhododendron, by the ribbons the sucked mint loosed
                on the air,
by the treasonous gold-leaved passage of season, and you

from me/child/from me/

from . . . not mother: no:
but the weather that would hold you: yes:

hothouse you to fattest blooms: keep you in mild unceasing rain, and the fixed
    stations of heat: like a pedalled note: or the held
        breath: sucked in, and stay: yes:
stay

but: no: not done: can't be:

the doe lay dead: she could
do nothing:

the dead can mother nothing . . . nothing
but our sight: they mother that, whether they will or no:

they mother our looking, the gap the tongue prods when the tooth is missing,
  when
        fancy seeks the space.

The doe lay dead: yes: and at a distance, with her legs up and frozen, she tricked
        our vision: at a distance she was
           for a moment no deer
at all

but two swans: we saw two swans
    and they were fighting
    or they were coupling
        or they were stabbing the ground for some prize
           worth nothing, but fought over, so worth *that*, worth
the fought-over glossiness: the morning's fragile-tubed glory.

And this is the soul: like it or not. Yes: the soul comes down: yes: comes
into the deer: yes: who dies: yes: and in her death twins herself into swans:
fools us with mist and accident into believing her newfound finery

and we are not afraid
though we should be

and we are not afraid as we watch her soul fly on: paired

as the soul always is: with itself:
  with others.
                Two swans . . .

Child. We are done for
in the most remarkable ways.

Brad Kessler

One Reader's Digest

Toward a Gastronomic Theory of Literature

The first novel I ever read with gusto was Pearl Buck's *The Good Earth*. I was a late reader and a slow reader and *The Good Earth* seemed, to a child at least, a particularly daunting book. The John Day hardback came with a brick-colored cover (mine had no dust jacket) with a typeface meant to mimic Chinese characters. The pages were yellowed and deckle-edged. The book looked exceedingly thick. *The Good Earth* — which won a Pulitzer in 1932 — followed the fortunes of a peasant farmer named Wang Lung in prerevolutionary China. Somewhere at the outset of the story, Wang Lung and his family nearly starve to death. The rain doesn't come; the crops fail. Wang grows appallingly thin (we can see his bones). He digs a few moldy beans from earth and devours them — but the famine only gets worse. Soon there's no food at all. I remember reading these pages with a terrible appetite. I lay in the comfort of an American suburb, the cabinets filled, TV in the other room; yet for those moments, lost in the pages of Pearl Buck, Wang Lung's hunger seemed to leak off the page and lodge itself directly in my stomach, as if it were me, and not Wang Lung, who couldn't find a thing to eat. His hunger became *mine*. Some chapters later, when Wang finally eats a handful of hot rice, and then wheat bread folded around a sprig of garlic, I could barely contain myself. I ran to the kitchen, ravenous, ransacking cupboards for white rice, jasmine tea, bags of take-out noodles (anything that seemed Chinese) trying to fill *myself* with what Wang Lung lacked. I didn't know what to do next: read or eat.

Reading *The Good Earth* had a lasting effect. For since then, reading and hunger seemed somehow inextricably bound. What I didn't know then, was *how* they were connected, only that filling oneself up with words seemed almost an alimentary activity. The novels I gravitated toward, consequently, all had a lot of eating in them. They were books in which the author rewarded his or her figures every few pages with a supper or a light repast; where, every few chapters, characters broke from the hard work of being written about, and enjoyed a meal. How — and more important *what* — they ate seemed of paramount importance. And though I've read a thousand scenes in fiction since *The Good Earth*, the ones that stay in mind the most involve eating. Names of characters fade. Plots are forgotten (even the point of the novel itself). But the meals, strangely, persist. I recall absolutely nothing of Trollope, for example, except that somewhere, in one of his Barsetshire novels, a barrister or a clergyman (I have no idea which) sits down in a grubby establishment and orders a mutton chop and a pint of sherry. Likewise, most of Henry James has slipped from mind, except for a particular oyster saloon on Seventh Avenue in *Washington Square*, where the gold-digging Morris consumes a steaming bowl of oyster stew. These scenes — the plate of mutton chops, the glass of sherry, the oyster stew — remain as vivid as a still life by Chardin. Forever colorful. Forever fresh. Forever, seemingly, edible.

Characters in novels seldom require food to survive, E. M. Forster famously observed. They hunger, as we do in life, for each other, "but our equally constant longing for . . . lunch . . . never gets reflected." Fortunately, Forster overstated the case. For there've always been authors who "reflected" quite a good deal of lunch and dinner, breakfast, and dessert. Rabelais, Flaubert, Dumas spring immediately to mind (Dumas even wrote his own *Dictionaire du Cuisine*). But the gastrorealists weren't limited to the French. Cervantes fed Sancho Panza every few chapters. Hemingway was never chary with the details of lunch (Nick Adams's thickly sliced onion sandwiches, flapjacks slathered with apple butter). Joyce's characters enjoyed squab pigeon pasties, porksteaks, nutty gizzards, and fried hencod's roes. Burnt kidneys, fried bread, and cold pig's trotters — the list goes on.

A friend once pointed out that every good novel she'd ever read opened with a food scene in the very first or second chapter. I doubted this was the case, but then, upon investigation, found she wasn't far off: many of the greatest novels did, indeed, have a banquet, a breakfast, or a dinner in the first few pages of the book. In *Madame Bovary* food appears on page ten (a baked veal); on page twenty-four (clotted cream and stewed pears); then three pages later (an underdone leg of mutton, old cider). But all this is just an appetizer for Charles and Emma's wedding feast, which appears a short time later, and whose comestibles are limned in full by Flaubert: fricassees, stewed veals, dishes of yellow cream "that trembled with the least shake of the table," a roast suckling pig "flanked by four chitterlings with sorrel."

Likewise, hardly has *Anna Karenina* begun, when Stepan Arkadyevich and the rather prudish Levin unfold their napkins in a Saint Petersburg restaurant. Stepan asks for not one dozen, nor two . . . but *three* dozen oysters. And what kind of oysters? he asks.

"Flensburg," the waiter tells him, "we've no Ostend."

"Flensburg will do, but are they fresh?"

"Only arrived yesterday."

Stepan then orders: clear soup with vegetables, turbot with a Beaumarchais sauce, a roast beef, capons, preserved fruit, and Parmesan cheese for after.

And to drink? Tolstoy's characters debate for a moment and finally agree: the Cachet blanc champagne with the oysters. A classic Chablis for table wine.

In *Moby Dick* food arrives in the first chapter as well (broiled, buttered fowl "judgematically salted and peppered"). Nine pages on, Ishmael eats his supper at the Spouter Inn (meat and potatoes, dumplings, and scalding tea), breakfast the very next morning (beefsteak), and finally, in Nantucket, before Ishmael and Queequeg *even set foot* on the Pequod, they enter the famous Try Pots (in a chapter called "Chowder") where they eat the soup of the same name. "It was made," Melville waxes, "of small juicy clams, scarcely bigger than hazelnuts, mixed with pounded ship biscuits, and salted pork cut up into little flakes! the whole enriched with butter and plentifully seasoned with pepper and salt." One gets the feeling, Melville was definitely a pepper man.

The point I'm trying to make is that all this eating happens quite early — the first chapter or so — which raises the question: What function do these early meals serve, if any, in the narrative? Are they merely *descriptive*? Do they simply set the scene? Or like an hors d'oeuvre, do they stimulate the reader's appetite for the larger meal ahead: namely the novel itself.

Food in fiction engages all the reader's senses (taste, touch, feel, sight, and smell). So putting a meal up front, early on, might very well stimulate the salivary glands. Food also lends a concreteness, a specificity, a round tactile feel, like an apple in hand. But what, if any, are the limits to eating in fiction? Could you put too much of it in? Would the reader suffer a syntactical indigestion? On the other hand, if you left eating out altogether, would you not starve your characters, and your readers in turn, and leave all parties peaked with hunger?

I want to mention one other example of eating in an early chapter, and this from *The Odyssey*. I'd like to pay particular attention to *The Odyssey*, because the epic is, in a sense, *the* Ur-novel, the template for all novels that came after. Unlike those other books of antiquity — the Old and New Testament — which were meant, less to entertain than to instruct or inspire (or browbeat), *The Odyssey* was primarily entertainment. It was music. It was poetry — only last was it inspiration, or counsel. Though *The Odyssey*, we're told, was sung aloud in dactylic hexameter, the architecture of the epic has the sensibility of a novel. Rather: all succeeding novels have vestiges of the epic still clinging to their pages (Borges called the novel a *degeneration* of the epic). At any rate, for my purposes, I'm claiming *The Odyssey* as a work of fiction, and true to the food-in-the-first-scene theory, eating begins early in the epic.

Hardly has *The Odyssey* begun, when Athena, disguised in human form, arrives in Ithaca at Odysseus' home. Telemachus, Odysseus' distraught son, invites the goddess inside for a meal, and before they speak, according to custom, Athena is offered food. The meal serves as both the entrée into the epic, and a kind of offering to the goddess, the muses, and the reader (or listener as the case may be), inviting them all to sit down to wine, meat, and bread, before they launch into the long poem.

But the eating in *The Odyssey* doesn't end there. Nor does it end in the next chapter or in the next. Or anytime at all, really. Some *forty-two* meals occur in the epic. Since there's twenty-four chapters, or "books" in *The Odyssey*, this averages almost two meals per chapter. Fielding called *The Odyssey* the "eatingest epic," and the meals there are no light affairs, no small Greek salads, or tiramasalata on pita. In *The Odyssey* they eat barley, oats, hot loaves of bread, honeyed wine. They eat barbecued backbones, beef, mutton, goat, venison, pork, wild boar. They eat sheep cheese, goat cheese, young porkers, roasted thigh bones, apples, figs, grapes, the famous goat sausages "sizzling with fat and blood" that Odysseus, disguised as a beggar, fights for upon his return to Ithaca. Even the adversaries eat in the epic: Polyphemus (the Cyclops) dines on human brains and bones and washes them down, alternately, with sheep milk and wine. The Lystergonians eat humans. The gods of course eat ambrosia.

The typical Odyssean meal involves not only descriptions of food, but also details of their preparation:

> They quartered (the heifer) quickly, cut the thighbones out, and all according to custom wrapped them round in fat, a double fold

sliced clean and topped with strips of flesh. And the old king burned these over dried split wood, and over the fire poured out glistening wine, while young men at his side held five pronged forks. Once they'd burned the bones and tasted the organs, they sliced the rest into pieces, spitted them on skewers and raising point to the fire, broiled all the meats. They roasted the prime cuts, pulled them off the spits and sat down to the feast while ready stewards saw to rounds of wine.

So the question is: Why so much eating? Did the meals serve as introductions to stories? Did they frame the scenes? Did they act as a spur, each meal leading to the next? Let's consider one theory. Almost all the stories in *The Odyssey* are told around the table. Only after his meal in King Alcinous' court, does Odysseus begin to tell his tale of the sea adventures (the Cyclops, Circes, the sirens, Schylla and Charybdis, etc). This is the heart, for some, of the epic, and we should remember it is told *en table*, as the banqueters sit spellbound for five chapters (76 pages) until Odysseus comes to the end of his saga. Afterwards, the diners decamp, in the early hours of the morning, only to return the next day for more food and more stories.

The table in *The Odyssey* acts as the locus, not only for food, but also for stories. The word "table" comes from the Latin *tabula*: a board, plank, a flat slab "intended to receive an inscription or an account." So the table, in its own etymology, is a place for recording, for inscription, for "accounts" — not only accounts in the mathematical sense, but accounts in the narrative sense as well. The board or plank turned horizontal is a dining table, and it serves the same purpose. The table is, at any rate, an ancient framing device for storytelling. The mead hall in *Beowulf*, the Round Table of the Arthurian tales, the inn of the *Canterbury Tales* all, in varying degrees, or by suggestion, serve as the frame for stories. The Passover table is the stage for either, or both, the Seder tales or the Last Supper narrative (depending on one's perspective, or religion). The link between table and account might well have something to do with *when* stories were told, or *when* it was deemed appropriate to tell them. For the troubadour and the bard and the harpist historically entertained after a meal, around the candlelight, when the body was sated and it was time to feed the imagination. (Interestingly, an old superstition in Iraq warns that, to tell a story during the daylight hours was to risk growing horns).

If we take the etymology of "table" one step further, we find its diminutive in the Old French, *tableau*: a striking scene, a picturesque representation, produced unexpectedly and *dramatically*. Here too, we find drama in the very meaning of the word "table." Certainly artists (painters, playwrights) have employed the table as a framing device and backdrop, the meal as the canvas around which figures come and go. Turgenev's novella *First Love* is told around the table between aging gentlemen. The principal action in Joyce's *The Dead* occurs around the Christmas table at the Misses Morkan (among goose, ham, spiced beef, red and yellow jelly, blancmange, Smyrna figs, custard, etc. . . .). The dining table figures often in Chekhov, in both the dramas and the short stories. The table *and* the meal *is* the centerpiece of Isak Dinesen's wonderful *Babette's Feast*. Meals are magnets; they draw people together. They are dramas, in fiction as in life. They also follow a strict narrative logic, which roughly mimics Aristotle's rule for a three-act drama: beginning (appetizer), middle (entrée) and end (dessert). If we look at the meal from a metabolic standpoint, the Aristotle model might read something like this: development (eating), crisis (digestion), and denouement (defecation). Or this:

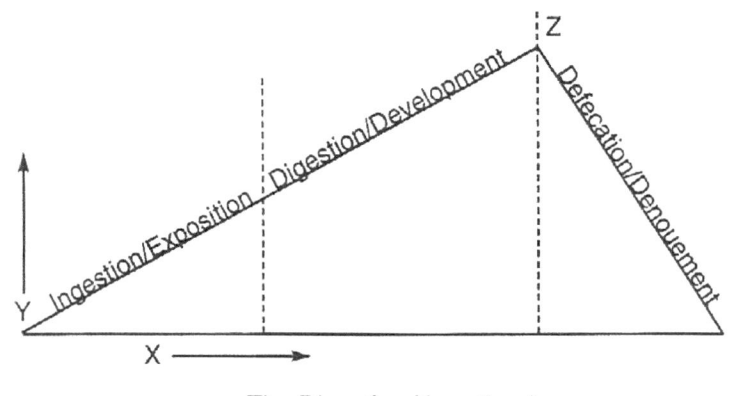

The Digestive-Narrative Arc
X = Time
Y = Drama

    Few other writers in the twentieth century feature as many dinner parties in their fiction as does Virginia Woolf. Odd, it seems, since, on the surface, Woolf strikes us as a rather peckish author, a gastrominimalist to be sure. Some biographers (though not all) suggest Woolf was anorexic. Yet despite her personal eating habits — or perhaps because of them — the table for Woolf is a fertile place, a place where people imbibe mainly of each other. And while many of her books pass with slender a mention of food, she was too skilled a writer *not* to tell us, from time to time, what people actually ate.

    Her two most celebrated novels, *Mrs. Dalloway* and *To the Lighthouse*, feature a meal at their very center. In *Dalloway* the novel's action builds to Clarissa's London dinner party, and in *Lighthouse* the action empties from the supper at the Ramsays' summer house in the Hebrides. In both cases, the meals serve as centerpieces, the place in which the drama is distilled.

The narrative in *Lighthouse* is told from many different points of view, from Mrs. Ramsay, Mr. Ramsay, the children (Cam, Prue, Andrew, etc.), Lilly Briscoe the painter, William Bankes the biologist, Charles Tansley "the atheist"—to name a few. We pop in and out of their heads, as they move about the house in the Hebrides, in the garden, the drawing room, the halls, the narrative passing from one to the other, like a baton, out to the beach, the bluffs, and beyond in the dunes, each character in his or her own orbit, separated by the nearly transparent membrane of his or her own consciousness. The whole action of the first part of *Lighthouse* can be read as a gradual movement toward the table, toward the meal, where the constellations briefly come into alignment and the disparate consciousnesses meld through the communion of the meal. What brings them all together is the main course, a Boeuf en Daub, Mrs. Ramsay's grandmother's recipe, cooked by the servants and overseen by Mrs. Ramsay herself. When the Boeuf en Daub is unveiled at the table, all the subterranean conflicts, intrigues, antagonisms, are briefly heightened, and then put aside, as each separate party partakes of the same flesh. "An exquisite scent of olives and oil and juice rose from the great brown dish," Woolf writes,

> as Marthe, with a little flourish, took the cover off. The cook had spent three days over that dish. And she must take great care, Mrs. Ramsay thought, diving into the soft mass, to choose a specially tender piece for William Bankes. And she peered into the dish, with its shiny walls and its confusion of savory brown and yellow meats and its bay leaves and its wine, and thought, This will celebrate the occasion—for what could be more serious than the love of man for woman, what more commanding, more impressive, bearing in its bosom the seeds of death.

The "occasion" is the imminent engagement of two minor characters at the dinner table (Minta Doyle and Paul Rayley). But the occasion is also the engagement of all of them together, there in a house in summer in the Hebrides: By eating the roast, they become one body. For a novel that explores the separateness of consciousness, the table is the one place where all can commune, where all bodies connect, through food. The same might also be said for *Mrs. Dalloway*. For all the action in that novel leads to the dinner party, at the end of the book, where Clarissa and her old friends Sally Seton and Peter Walsh, and dozens of others (including the prime minister) come together to partake in each other, as well as chicken in aspic, salmon (underdone), soup, ice cream. *What* they eat is not as important as the fact that they *do* eat, that they manage, after all the aloneness and antagonisms and pain and separateness, they persist and find a way to put food in themselves. We know, for Woolf, this has special meaning, as there were times in her life when she couldn't eat at all, and was hospitalized by her illness. Just as she struggled with food and eating (and staying alive) she managed, like her characters, to find celebration, even beauty, in food and eating, despite herself.

"It is a triumph" the aloof scientific Mr. Bankes announces in *Lighthouse* after he has eaten the Boeuf en Daub. "He had eaten it attentively. It was rich; it was tender. It was perfectly cooked." The meat has melted his previous standoffishness toward Mrs. Ramsay and the others. The meal, therefore, is as much social triumph for Mrs. Ramsay, as an epicurean one.

So what is this Boeuf en Daub that serves as the centerpiece in *Lighthouse*? My *Larousse Gastronomique* has four recipes for Daub de Boeuf, and unlike Mrs. Ramsay's recipe, none call for olives. Larousse says a Boeuf de Daub is best prepared in a *daubiere*, which is a kind of casserole of stoneware or earthenware or copper. It is, in other words, a pot for braising meat and vegetable, a melting pot, a kind of witches' cauldron, if you will. The feminist critic Alice Glenny suggests that the big round pot, with its mingled meats, represents a pregnant belly in which one flesh is indistinguishable from another. The stew pot alludes to the mother's gift — and specifically Mrs. Ramsay's gift — of feeding from her own body both the fetuses of her children, and all the sucklings around her, namely the communicants at the table, both male and female. Glenny argues that Mrs. Ramsay, in this regard, is a kind of fertility goddess, a Demeter, or Ceres, and the pot of meat suggests as well her sexual-marital unity with Mr. Ramsay.

That may be a lot to read into one pot roast, yet it is fair to say that food for Woolf, as with most other writers, is freighted with meaning. Just as in life, food in fiction signifies. It means more than itself. It is symbolic. It opens doors to double and triple meaning. The Invisible Man of Ralph Ellison's eponymous classic buys a hot baked yam from a stove cart on a cold night in Harlem, and the yam is as packed with meaning as it is with pulp. Eating it openly, on the street, is an act of defiance and liberation for the narrator. All the food in Ellison's novel has a semiotic quality, the cabbage soup in Miss Mary's house, the pork chop and grits breakfast he disdains (to prove he has risen above his poor southern black upbringing) while secretly longing. All of the food of his race haunts him as a kind of defeat, a humiliation. To shame his former mentor, the Uncle-Tomish Bledsoe, the narrator fantasizes about flogging him in public with a chain of raw chitterlings, shouting to the world that Bledsoe is "a sneaking chitterling lover," chewing hog jowls and pig ears and black-eyed peas on the sly.

On the simplest level, the yam and Miss Mary's cabbage soup serve as memory triggers in *Invisible Man*. The smell of the hot yam, bubbling in its own juice, floods Ellison's narrator with another time and place. ("I stopped as though struck by a shot," writes Ellison, ". . . At home we'd bake them in the hot coals of the fireplace, had carried them cold to school for lunch; munched them secretly, squeezing the sweet pulp from the soft peel as we hid from the teacher behind the largest book . . . candied, or baked in a cobbler, deep-fat fried, in a pocket of dough, or roasted with pork . . . the time seemed endlessly expanded.") For Ellison, food, as in life, is a transport, a vehicle for nostalgia. Smell, the librarian of the senses, stores in its stacks every odor we've ever sniffed, and leaves it there, preserved, unawakened, until we have cause to experience it again. In a way, when we talk about "craving" a certain kind of food, we're really talking about memory, about wanting to relive the past *through* food. The most celebrated unpacking of memory through food occurs, of course, in Proust. His madeleine soaked in a mouthful of lime-blossom tea awakens an entire world of memory — seven books worth. A madeleine is but a small fluted cookie made of flour, butter, eggs, and sugar (with the addition of vanilla or salt, depending on the recipe). Imagine what Proust could have done on a less meager diet, A. J. Liebling famously quipped. What kind of masterpiece might he have produced on a dozen oysters, a bowl of clam chowder, a pair of lobsters, a Long Island duck?

If food triggers memories in literature, if it can't help but be semiotic, what does it commonly signify? Carnality, appetite, desire — all the usual subjects. The perishability and baseness of the body. And, of course, sex. Eating involves putting things into our bodies, and usually when things get put into our bodies (through whichever orifice) or come out of our bodies (through whichever orifice) the activity is done in private. Eating transgresses the boundary. That it is done in public is a relatively modern phenomenon (in some countries eating in mixed company in public is still taboo). In fiction, as in life, people can be a bit squeamish about eating in front of others. It raises uncomfortable issues of body image, craving, sexuality; so it's not surprising that some authors are uncomfortable with the whole affair of eating. Some writers never have their characters eat, in public *or* in private.

Hardly anyone ever eats in an Austen novel, for example. Though there are balls and dinners and breakfasts aplenty, we never catch a Lizzie or a Jane or an Emma actually putting anything into her mouth. It's not that Austen characters are underfed; we're told about suppers all the time. But when they *do* eat, it's done furtively, hidden from the view of the reader. On the very rare occasion that Austen does mention food, it is something usually unappetizing, a plate of "cold meat" or a slightly putrified haunch of venison.

Most of the houses inhabited by Austen's characters have a specially designated "breakfast room." We hear about them in passing, in Netherfield Park, Northanger Abbey, Mansfield Park, Longbourne, but we never actually *see* breakfast. Here is the closest we get, in *Northanger Abbey*, when Catherine takes breakfast at the Tilneys':

> [Captain Tilney's] anxiety for her comfort—his continuous solicitations that she would eat, and his often-expressed fears of her seeing nothing to her taste—though never in her life before had she beheld half such variety on a breakfast table—made it impossible for her to forget for a moment that she was a visitor.

What, pray tell, did she behold on the table? Who's to know. When Austen illustrates a table, it's usually not the food she focuses on, but the china.

"The elegance of the breakfast set forced itself on Catherine's notice," Austen writes in *Northanger Abbey*,

> ... luckily, (the tea seat) had been the General's choice. He was enchanted by her approbation of his taste, confessed it to be neat and simple, thought it right to encourage the Manufacture of his country; and for his part, to his uncritical palate, the tea was as well flavored from the clay of Staffordshire, as from that of Dresden or Sevres.

One clue to Austen's food attitude appears in *Emma*. Miss Bates confides that her niece has little appetite in the morning: "Dear Jane," she frets. "She really eats nothing—makes such a shocking breakfast, you would be quite frightened ... how little she eats." As readers, we feel quite the same: frightened by how little *all* her characters eat. But the question remains: why does Austen never mention the particular "articles of plate"? Is eating inherently shameful, something best left off the page, like defecating, or changing underwear?

Certainly shame and eating have a long-linked history in Western culture. All the way back in Eden, when Adam and Eve ate the forbidden fruit (folk tradition has it as an apple) their immediate reaction was not delight or satiation, but humiliation: a crushing recognition of the exigencies of their bodies. Tellingly, they react by covering, not their mouths — the organs of their eating — but their genitalia. The connection at any rate is clear: Eating equals *shame*. Eating equals *sexuality*.

From Socrates to Descartes it's the same story: The body is bestial, unclean, base. The mind pure, spiritual. Socrates urged his acolytes to escape the body: ("as long as we have a body and our soul is fused with such an evil, we shall never adequately attain . . . the truth"). The body was to be conquered, controlled, governed; it was dangerous, unpredictable, a kind of *other*. Aristotle, for one, thought the body inherently female and the mind (surprise) as male. So women's bodies *especially* needed to be governed (because, among other things, of what they provoked in men). Denying the body through fasting was one path toward purity, just as celibacy was another. Christian iconography only affirmed that denial: Christ in all his imagery hasn't an ounce of adipose. (Contrast Him with Buddha Shakyumani, who is always portrayed as sated and content in his folds of body fat.)

The argument against the body found its full flowering in Victorian England. The critic Anna Silver maintains that Victorian upper-class women were supposed to appear unconcerned with food. They were to look sylph-like, and forced themselves into thinness through starvation, corsets, bodices, and stays. Slight, pale women were associated with the upper class (and spirituality), while large fleshy women suggested the lower class (and carnality). Silver argues that anorexia nervosa first appeared in upper- and middle-class Victorian households as a response to the idealization of the thin, etherealized woman. At the same time, rejecting the bounty of the table was one of the few avenues of protest open to young women: They could deny the patriarchy by simply refusing its food.

If Victorian women were supposed to display a demure appetite, it serves to reason that Victorian women *writers* would abstain from excess *writing* about food. It was one thing for Dickens or Hardy to wax about beefsteak or pudding, but quite another for George Eliot or Jane Austen. On the other side of the Atlantic, Emily Dickinson wrote over and over about her sacred hunger, but was quite happy to subsist, as she writes, on crumbs. And yet gastrominimalism, strangely, was not limited to women writers alone. How much food is ever eaten in Joseph Conrad, for example, or Nathaniel Hawthorne? Men stick cigars in their mouths all the time in Henry James, but rarely do they put anything else between their lips.

As for the characters in nineteenth-century novels, big eaters are generally associated with moral feebleness. Think of the gluttonous Gentleman of the Board in Dickens's *Oliver Twist*. Those who renounce food or eat sensibly — even better those who have no appetite at all (Kafka's Hunger Artist) — are superior, even noble. Chekhov employs food repeatedly to underscore the crassness and brutality of the aristocracy. At moments of great pique and passion, when his figures are on the brink of an enlightened thought or a grand emotion, Chekhov always has some brute stumble in and undercut the sentimentality with his stomach. There's the sexton in the short story "In the Ravine" who, "petrified with enjoyment," eats an entire jar of large-grained caviar (to everyone's horror) at a funeral. In the same story, a young woman has just lost her only child (scalded to death by a jealous rival); another priest "lifting his fork on which there was a salted mushroom" exhorts dismissively: "Don't grieve for the babe; such is the kingdom of heaven." In "Lady with Lapdog," after Gurev seduces the married Anna, he slips out of bed and greedily devours a watermelon while Anna sheds tears over what they've done. Later, when Gurev realizes he's actually in love with Anna, he's about to confess his great secret to a friend.

> "If only you knew what a charming woman I met in Yalta!" he confides after a Moscow dinner.
> "Dmitry Dmitrich!" the friend replies, surprised.
> "Yes," says Gurev.
> "You were quite right, the sturgeon was just a little off."

I want to look briefly at one more gastrominimalist: Let us sail swiftly now, across the Atlantic, toward another century and another author, who had an uneasy relationship with both food and women. We're in the 1930s, outside Jefferson, Mississippi, in a culture almost as coded and proscribed as Austen's. We could probably search high and low in almost any of Faulkner's works and find hardly a biscuit to nibble on, but I want to focus, briefly, on one of his best known works: *Light in August*.

It always puzzled me why an author as engaging of all the senses could get food (*and* women) so wrong. For such a descriptive author, Faulkner turns downright clamp-mouthed when food appears on his pages. To be fair, Faulkner does feed his characters, but he suffers, like Austen, from a nervous stomach. His characters smoke and drink with gusto, but eat grudgingly, almost as if it were a duty. And rarely, if ever, do we see *what* they eat.

There are several short meals in *Light in August*: the supper and breakfast the pregnant Lena eats at the Armstids' on her way to Jefferson; the bagged lunch Byron Bunch tries to offer Joe Christmas at the lumber mill; the dinner in the seedy luncheonette where Joe Christmas goes with his stepfather, Mr. McEachern. In each of these, we're never told *what* they eat. Here is a typical Faulknerian description of a meal:

> The food which McEachern ordered was simple: quickly prepared and quickly eaten . . . as soon as he laid down his knife and fork, McEachern said, come, already getting down from his stool.

Faulkner glosses over his meals because, among other things, food in his work is exclusively the domain of women. Women prepare it; women offer it; women eat it. Consequently, food seems beyond Faulkner's orbit of understanding. Yet food signifies something much darker for Faulkner. There are three women in Joe Christmas's life in *Light in August*: his stepmother, Mrs. McEachern; his waitress girlfriend, Bobbie Allen; his spinster lover, Joanna Burden. Each woman is a provider of food. But the food they provide comes with a cost. In each case, the food is sexualized, feminine, threatening, ("corrupting" *qua* Socrates). The act of desiring and eating woman's food is similar to the act of desiring woman's bodies. In both cases, the carnality is shameful.

The shame begins early for Joe Christmas. After a day of being whipped by his stepfather for not learning his catechism, the young Christmas is brought food by his stepmother, the preacher's wife. She steals into Christmas's bedroom with a tray of food "prepared in secret and offered in secret," made for the boy "against the will of the stepfather." The young Christmas takes the tray out of the woman's hands, walks to the corner, and dumps the food defiantly on the floor. He will not be feminized by the food. He will not eat the poisoned apple.

Later, Christmas lives in a shack behind the decaying mansion of the Yankee spinster, Joanna Burden. Christmas, who is half-white, half-black, an orphan, a runaway, sneaks into the spinster's house at night, lured there like a feral cat, by plates of food left out for him by the older white woman. Night after night, he eats secretly, shamefully, until, emboldened, he creeps upstairs to Joanna Burden's bedroom. Instead of surprise or shock (or fear), Joanna Burden has expected him all along; for once Christmas has taken her food in the cover of darkness, he will take her as well, both carnal acts (eating and sex) equally secretive, equally shameful. Yet Christmas, in the end, must reject both food and women, and he does so violently. When he enters

Joanna Burden's kitchen for the last time, he smashes plates of food against the wall, one by one. Interestingly, the only time we're told the specifics about the food is not when they're being eaten, but when they're being tossed. "Woman's muck" Christmas seethes, pitching plates across the room. "Ham, beans or spinach," he says, identifying each as he hurls them. "Something with onions, potatoes . . . beets." After he tosses the food, he smacks and punches Joanna Burden and then burns her house down. A dyspeptic moment to be sure. One wonders: was the food *that* bad?

Sometime after I discovered my preference for the gastrorealists, I began perusing cookbooks. If I wanted to read about food, why slog through all those scenes and plot twists in novels, just to find a sentence or two where someone actually eats? Why not cut to the chase? So I bought *Larousse Gastronomique*, the bible of French cookery, with its 1100 pages, and four-color photographs of *Hare Pâté* or *Eel en brochette*. I read Fanny Farmer and Irma Rombauer. I delved into *The Roman Cookery of Apicius* (the earliest acknowledged cookbook); I even read Platina, the Renaissance epicurean writer whose *On Right Pleasure and Good Health* was an eye opener (if not exactly a mouth waterer. His recipe for "Peacock Cooked So It Seems to Be Alive" is more decorative than appetizing). I read also the literary gourmands — Anthelme Brillat-Savarin's classic *The Physiology of Taste*, M. F. K. Fisher, Alice Toklas. Yet by and large the cookbooks themselves were disappointing. The plots were predictable (they always followed the same outline: appetizer, soup, vegetable, fish, meat, dessert). The characters (usually first person) were alternately charming, officious, or technocratic. Though cookbooks had a narratology all their own, they lacked the forward motion, the engine, the drama that food in novels offered. Oddly, the nakedness of the food itself in cookbooks, the frankness with which it was discussed, unadorned by plot or scenery, made the food seem scientific, clinical. It made the food, well . . . unpalatable. Meals limned in cookbooks did not arouse the same kind of appetite and longing that reading about them in fiction did. Was a meal surrounded by a story, then, more enticing? Did the narrative, the withholding, the slow striptease of plot and character, actually increase one's appetite? Did all the pages of noneating only make the eating seem more irresistible (as in *The Good Earth* when, after all those pages of hunger, Wang Lung, finally eats)? Either way, it seemed something enfolded or wrapped inside a narrative tasted better than simply the raw thing.

Besides, cookbooks read less like novels than collections of small, odd poems. Recipes, with their dramatic line breaks, their concern for metrics and timing (prosody), seemed to share more with poetry than narrative fiction. And a recipe, like a poem, has its own internal combustion, its own logic; a good one creates something greater than the sum of its parts. I read my *Larousse* that way, at any rate, as an anthology of odd poems translated from another language, each entry an ode. Enigmatic as a haiku. Here, for example, is a fragment (chosen almost at random) from a recipe for "Garden Warblers in the Manner of Father Fabri" — the line breaks are mine:

> Garden Warblers in the Manner of Father Fabri
>
> Put a piece of Foie gras
> The size of a walnut
> Studded with a piece of truffle
> inside each warbler
> Brown briskly in sizzling butter
>
> simply to set the surface.

Another reads like this:

> Irish Smoked Herrings
>
> Wash and dry the Herrings
> Cut off the heads.
> Split the fish in half,
> lengthwise.
> Spread them very flat
> in a deep dish,
> cover with whisky and set light to them.
> When the whisky has all burned away
> and the flame extinguished,
> The herrings are ready to eat.

They were wonderful recipes, at any rate, read side by side with the food poems of Frances Ponge, Pablo Neruda, Ogden Nash, D. H. Lawrence, or Gertrude Stein (all of whom were gastrorealists). Were the recipes in *Larousse* so very different from William Carlos Williams's "This Is Just to Say" (This is just to say / I have eaten / the plums / that were in / the icebox // and which / you were probably / saving / for breakfast // Forgive me / they were delicious / so sweet / and so cold.)?

A writer is forever trying to get his reader to taste. Taste my world, he says, smell it, ingest it. A novelist involves himself with the raw materials of the world just as a cook does with an onion, a carrot, an egg. Both the cook and the writer season and simmer their material for good long stretches, until they have accomplished something worthy (hopefully) of intake. Readers, alas, are finicky. They might taste a morsel, a sentence here, a chapter there. The trick is to convince them to stick around for the entire meal. The novelist's job (like the poet's) is to reduce experience into a fine distillation, what Rilke called "the smallest units of language." Just as a *sous*-chef reduces his stock, the writer must reduce his vision into a teaspoon of life, highly condensed, a tonic so potent that, when taken, it transforms us.

I think the real link between food and literature is that they both satisfy, not only an appetite, but a *hunger*. A hunger for words. A hunger for the lives of others, a hunger to transcend our own small selves and enter the bodies of others — different from us, yet the same — across the divide of centuries or class or culture or gender or race. Across consciousness itself. Food is the great leveler. We all need it equally as much as the other. When I read *The Good Earth* I didn't know it at the time, but I hungered not only for the food that Wang Lung lacked, but also for a connection to another time and place outside the proscribed suburb I'd grown up in. That was the transformative thing about the book, about any good book: that it transports us, that it fills in the voids, the emptiness, the terrible appetite in all of us.

"Ink runs from the corners of my mouth," the poet Mark Strand writes. "There is no happiness like mine. I have been eating poetry." But the same can be said about any good literature. We put a book inside ourselves and digest the edible bits, and jettison the rest, and if the story (or poem) is good, if it is honest, if it offers us some consolation or way of being in the world, it becomes, like bread, a part of us.

Colleen Kinder

One Bright Case of Idiopathic Cranofacial Erythema

I blamed the malady on my Irish side: the relatives who stared out from baby pictures like porcelain dolls. My mom's parents were immigrants, effortlessly proper in that just-hoping-to-blend-in-and-prosper kind of way, not to mention Catholic. Severely Catholic. When I read about "lace curtain Irish" in an American Studies course in college, my ancestors provided an instant visual.

My father's side, on the contrary, is a long line of American mutts, California-based for too many decades to trace back across the Atlantic. Dad grew up in a house with sandals, TV dinners, various pets, no religiously coded conduct rules. The paternal genes were more loosely bound: less Mass, more beach. I never considered them as carriers.

Until the night the loud speaker called my Dad.

"*Would the parents of the players please come out . . .*"

He and I were high in the bleachers, slumped against the wall, waiting for the Holy Angels basketball game to begin. We were not expecting a voice.

"Oh, geez." Dad obeyed the voice, rising to his feet.

I consider my father a self-assured man. He started a business; he gives a fine toast; he'll make small talk with a corn farmer as easily as a senator. But standing at half court, amidst the other parents, my dad turned the color of a pig roasted on charcoals. The blush spanned from shirt collar to balding spot. It dimmed none as Sister Kristen thanked the parents for their support, brownies, carpools — nothing remotely mortifying.

I looked down court, baffled. I'd have to revise my inheritances. Mom was the reason I wore SPF 45. Dad: why I sat in last rows.

"*Blushing*, though a fleeting episode, is experienced as an unwelcome public revelation of one's most private thoughts," wrote Angela Simon about a study at Morehead State University. "By 'blushing,' we specifically mean the transient feeling of warmth and/or skin color change associated with the occurrence of acute self-consciousness."

• •

Blushers remember a first time.

Sixth grade. Mrs. Mikulec had us keep journals in Language Arts class. I took the assignment further — on a plane to California.

Somewhere between Buffalo and San Francisco, a fleecy patch of clouds passed my oval window. Listening to the *Aladdin* sound track for about the seventeenth time, I was stirred by the coinciding songs of nature and Disney, and I opened my journal. There, I composed something that felt like true language art: my first metaphor.

Back at Christ the King, during a routine moment when boys shuffled through backpacks, girls clicked pens, Mrs. Mikulec called on me. She wanted me to share my latest journal entry with the class.

"No," I said.

"Yes, Colleen, it's lovely. Just read the plane part."

"No."

"C'mon, Colleen. They'll appreciate it."

"No way."

I had likened Delta flight 404 to a magic carpet ride.

"Yes. Get up here."

"No way."

"Colleen—"

One week had passed since the plane ride. One week, in the sixth grade scheme of growth, is enough to change your mind about everything. To forget your sanitary crush on Aladdin and start lusting after Jared Leto. A week is enough to decide you hate your own words. To regret language art.

"I *can't*."

There was a podium in the front of the room.

• •

Science explains it in this order:

    1. Situation causes shame or awkwardness.

    2. Adrenaline is released.

3. Heart rate climbs.
4. Breathing quickens.
5. Facial blood vessels dilate.
6. Blood flows to face.
7. More blood flows to face.
8. Face turns noticeably red.

1-7, in a word, as heard from the inside: *Foooosh*.

• •

It wasn't Aladdin. It wasn't the language art. It was her siege, multiplied by my resistance. A declaration to the public — the sixth grade class of Christ the King School — that reading in front of them was the last thing I desired to do. Then doing it.

I watched the rest happen from the back row. I watched over Peter's head, over Ellen's, over Brian's, watching them watch the color bloom, billow, spread to the outer reaches of my face, quitting only at the hairline. People think blushing is the fear of public attention. There's a difference between picking up the microphone, and the microphone plucking your name. The difference is a drastic crimson.

• •

Participants in a study reported that it takes one to four seconds for a blush to occur.

Or longer. Or five to ten seconds.

It depends on the subject. It depends on how the subject defines his or her blush. How he or she visualizes the color advancing across the cheeks — in a poof? as a streak? like the reindeer's nose? Imagination colors the blush, clocks the blush. Imagination reads panic, or shame, or both. That first flicker, or its aftermath? Which supplies the color, which the heat?

I wonder about this blush of the imagination. When the test participants paused, their number two pencils hanging above the multiple choice options — 1-4 seconds, 5-10 seconds, 11-25 seconds, half minute or more — what public shaming dislodged from memory? Was it any quicker in the reliving?

• •

Sister Karen Marie made a sport of calling on her most mortifyable pupils. There were three Colleens in my class of fifty. Two-thirds of these Colleens had the middle name Ann(e), two-thirds were red-headed, and three-thirds were prone to full-face blushes. I remember with pain the day "SKM" called Colleen McCarthy up to the chalkboard for some fill-in-the-blank-with-Bible-writers exercise. Colleen McCarthy did not know the Bible writer. SKM would not let her sit back down.

"Look," SKM said, alerting us to the sight of Colleen, fuming panic against the green chalkboard. "It's Christmas."

• •

When Angela Simon asked blushers how other people respond to their facial coloration, the most common response was: "They tease and try to get me to blush more."

• •

Willpower accomplished nothing. In fact, willpower like mine just stoked the fire. So I tried avoidance. I steered clear of any situation that might give my skin occasion to flare. I wore shorts under my plaid uniform skirt. I locked my journal in a small box under my bed and hid the key inside an unassuming stuffed animal beaver whose tail region I had slit open with a scissors. I did not raise my hand.

• •

Erythrophobia refers to a pathological fear of blushing. It means "fear of redness."

• •

Invisibility gets boring, particularly once puberty begins. I tried a new strategy. I set out to convince my public that they were rude to point out a blush. "That's the *worst* thing you can do," I'd chastise, on behalf of blushers everywhere. The problem was less in my cheeks, I'd realized, more in their eyes. So if they could just be a tad less *explicit* about their observations, notify me on a less frequent basis, in a less public fashion, then I might just see it was a breeze passing through my complexion. Passing. Breeze. Might. Just.

• •

Peter Drummond put fifty-six college women in a lab room in Murdoch University in Perth, Australia, and told them to sing aloud to "I Will Survive" by Gloria Gaynor for twenty seconds. After each woman sang, the experimenter entered the lab room to inform her whether or not she had blushed. At random, half of the women were told they blushed; the rest told they had not.

Each woman was then left alone for four minutes. After these four minutes, the experimenter returned and played a recording of "I Will Survive" with the subject's voice in the background. Her voice was louder than Gloria Gaynor's.

As hypothesized, Peter Drummond found that having given blushing feedback to those who scored high on the Blushing Propensity Scale increased blood flow to the face, progressively.

"These findings suggest that expecting to blush may become a self-fulfilling prophecy."

• •

You could boil my early development down to two traits. The first: ambition. Its underbelly: fear. Not raw fear, but the anticipatory sort.

$F^2 =$

Fear of my fear of not catching baseballs.

Fear of my fear of singing like a seagull.

Fear of my fear of holding babies too stiffly.

Then I grew up. I sophisticated. I specialized the ambition, got distance on the fear. By "got distance," I mean multiplied it out.

$F^3 =$ Fear of flare-up.

Fear of my fear of my fear of forgetting names.

Fear of my fear of my fear of my fear of sounding insincere.

Fear of my fear of my fear of clicking "*no*" when asked "*Save Changes?*"

What keeps all formulas intact is the blush — the awareness that I'm transparent. Faced with a public, for better or worse, I run the risk of lucidity. In the event of a falter, a curve ball, an unexpected, I have no place to handle it deeper than the plane of my skin.

• •

The awareness-raising campaign proved problematic. I was *telling* people they had the power to hike up the hue of my cheeks, learning, meanwhile, that even friends — even fellow Colleens — will lord such power. So why not deny it? I could accuse my audience of blush illiteracy. A *blush is not a blush is not a blush*. But rather:

a) Amusement. Church giggles smothered in a sleeve.

s) Surprise. Spider in the shower.

p) Panic. Wallet not in your pocket. Wallet not in your purse.

e) Empathy. Colleen McCarthy kept at the blackboard, called Christmas.

d) Deluge of Emotion X. The end of *Ghost*.

A blush can manifest anything. A blush can manifest something *good*. Hilarious! Something you don't know about. Even though roughly 87% of my blushes were born of raw humiliation, I prattled on about the spectrum. Not only because 13% was substantial, but because adolescence was teaching me things about self-esteem. About mine, it's quirks. That what I needed, for the time being, was a placebo.

• •

The Maybelline Blush Scale:

Flushed.Blush.Peach.Punch.Roseberry.Flame.Cherry.Wine.

• •

How do I know I blush?

I do. I know, because that much heat can't be white. How could it stay porcelain white? I know I blush because I've laid a hand against my cheek, afterwards, felt it calm like a light bulb. I know because my skin's thin and colorless; I've peeled it off after sunburns — sunburns that made strangers suck back their breath, sunburns I relished, under which I could smolder to high heaven. Only on sunburn days did I have room to imagine what it's like in another's pigment. With my skin scorched, I considered how I might act, given a guest pass to a Greek. How I could pull off just about anything, both cheeks dressed up. How, if all those F's got reciprocated, even for a couple hours, the base might be snuffed right out.

• •

<u>Flushed</u>: The windowless office of my teaching assistant Angus, who wore kilts and never sat down when discussing a work of Shakespeare.

<u>Blush</u>: "It says 'Card Rejected, ma'am. Insufficient funds?'"
<u>Peach</u>: Saying good-bye, to anyone — but men especially — on elevators.
<u>Punch</u>: Realizing, mid-afternoon, March 9, that I had not written a rent check since people were remarking "Happy New Year."
<u>Roseberry</u>: Fielding a nun's question — what religion are you?
<u>Flame</u>: At the table of the MFA workshop, hearing this essay's narrator critiqued.
<u>Cherry</u>: The subway car where I spilled a bag of plastic hangers, moving my belongings from Manhattan to Brooklyn by F trains.
<u>Wine</u>: The backdoor of a man who held eye contact too long, as he placed the *Collected Works of Hunter S. Thompson* into my hands. Fumble. Thump. *Fooosh*.

• •

How do I know I blush? Actually *color*? Peach then punch then flame, skipping cherry, to wine? I know because I've caught the aftermath in bathroom mirrors. I know I blush because there's a yearbook photo of my Dad and me dancing "The Twist" in the Holy Angels Father-Daughter Dance Competition. A long rash stretches from cheekbone to jaw.

I know I blush because there are precedents, photo evidence, physical heat. I know I blush by my audience. Because people do the favor of lowering their eyes. Because other people don't. Other people let you know what they see. Like I didn't feel the spike in temperature. Like I wasn't the furnace.

How do I know I blush? Pink, red, scarlet? Because that's a preposterous question. Because I've never entertained that I don't: it's that forcible. That visual. Each skin cell, an eye.

• •

Some claim that blushing is purposeful, from an evolutionary standpoint. Had it no purpose, humankind's red-faced would have been eliminated from the gene pool long ago — as, were, perhaps, a freak purple-faced people who never got their pale counterparts into bed.

Blushing clues onlookers in that the looked-upon person is suffering. The onlookers, then, have the prerogative to alleviate that suffering. Their options are many: crack joke, digress, flatter, point. You might call blushing involuntary communication — a tacit apology for a moment, a secret, a fumble, a fart. One individual feels the heat; the clan gleans the meaning; society is less contentious for all.

This evolutionary compromise must have been hammered out before language was. With a few words, a sensitive soul might have raised her hand and explained that there's pain in it for the spectator, too — even from the back row, the top bleacher. If evolution could come up with empathy, it should have done away with the blush. And when humans began chatting, their skin could have stopped saying so much.

• •

I didn't know any Koreans until college. The first Korean I made friends with didn't drink. "The Asian flush," he said, regretfully. I didn't know what that was, but doubted it could trump my blush. He explained that his face could flare up after a single drink. *Funny*, I thought. My people drink to cancel out the blush — to enable what would, in sober hours, stain the skin a guilty scarlet.

For my first three years of college, I kissed no one without a half-quart of alcohol in my bloodstream. I spent my Sundays hung-over, reminded over brunch what was comedic about my Saturday night. It wasn't until my senior year that a nice young man stopped by my dorm room — on a Tuesday — and we ended up horizontal on the futon.

"*Stay*," I told his ear, surprising myself.

"I should go," Chris said, sounding pliable.

He and I would quarrel about the conditions of our inaugural kiss for the next two years. I remembered this: me on top of Chris, playing predator — sober predator — for the first time in my life. Chris objects, having full memory of the previous Saturday evening, when he escorted me home from a toga party, to make out, until I got up to throw up.

• •

Studies of blushing have aimed to identify the personality traits of people with high "blushing propensity scores." In 1991, Leary and Meadows published a list of these traits.

The first was "embarassibility."

Then "interaction anxiousness."

Followed by "self esteem."

And finally "refinement."

Leary and Meadows explain that by "refinement," they mean "the degree to which one enjoys or is repulsed by crass, uncouth, and vulgar behavior."

. .

Early morning. Planned Parenthood. I'm excessively early, having applied the caution to "beat the line" too earnestly. I nap in the cabin of the car, hearing others pull up: women, girls, their friends. I hope this will be quick. I just need birth control.

But birth control requires an exam, my nurse tells me. I expected a warm woman; she is not warm. "We can't prescribe a pill without testing for herpes." I pause — then realize this is not a choice she's presenting. She gets tools. At the sight of these tools, my hands begin rubbing one another, rubbing hard. I wasn't expecting a test. My fingers knead my knuckles. Then knead palms. The talking stops. She doesn't give fair warning. The metal's cold.

"You need to relax."

My fingers knead my palms. "OK." My fingers knead my eyebrows. They knead into eyeballs. I try gripping the paper gown.

"You're *pushing*," my nurse sighs. "Relax."

I am told about pushing and am supposed to relax.

"Take a breath." I take a breath, as my nurse observes, no patience in her body language, no placing aside tools. I'm doing that thing that complicates her job: working myself up.

"*Relax.*"

Chris would know. He could read the braiding tension. He knew how to melt my resistance and pace us just behind it. This is what first love meant: a man literate in the exponential fears, patient enough to wait them out, saying nothing but what helped. Sweet-nothing placebos.

"You're crying." That's not a concern. That's the accusation of my nurse.

Sex was an obvious fear. It fell on the same side of the line as singing solos and driving go-carts and spelling aloud at bees. Performance — with audience; not work I could master alone. I learned about sex among Catholics, girls who aspired to bring virginity on their honeymoons. F had years to multiply, and did.

"I won't do this with you pushing," the nurse protested, tool down.

These are the moments I don't get people. These are the moments when not getting people feels like tightness just behind the eyebrows, an ice-cream headache, a tear pen. *Relax.* As if self-command were that simple, a linear path — brain to cheeks, brain to legs, brain to belief.

. .

103 *Colleen Kinder*

Hypothesis: Since previous research has proven that blushing phobics do not have a particularly low threshold for blushing or especially intense coloration, then fear of blushing may be fueled by mechanisms other than facial color, such as a biased interpretation of the communicative value of the blush.

Participants: Forty female undergraduates at Maastricht University.

Method: Females presented with vignettes of awkwardness (e.g. spilling wine, mistakenly picking up someone else's backpack and getting accosted by that person, spilling coffee).

Remuneration for participants: Chocolate bars.

Title of study: "Do Blushing Phobics Overestimate the Undesirable Communicative Effects of Their Blushing?"

Summary of conclusions: No.

• •

How I know I blush: Chris.

I just e-mailed, saying hey, writing about blushing, starting to wonder, as out of control as I think?

"When you blush, it's slow, steady and complete," replies Chris. "Pretty much the entire face to your ears."

He continues, "When you're trying to control it, when you're in a public situation, you usually stick your neck out and nod a little, with a bit of an 'oh my' smile on your mouth. Or you do a little nod and cough, your lips tight."

About here, I had to look away from the monitor.

• •

The most common strategy that participants of Angela Simon's study used to conceal a blush was: "try not to act embarrassed."

• •

"When it's a complete surprise, you say 'Whoah,' kind of laugh to cover up the blush, and sort of stumble a few steps back, your left hand on the crook of your right arm, and the right arm kind of fanning the air to get the embarrassing thing away."

About here, I wished I hadn't asked.

• •

Last try: humor.

"... Then I turned BRI-ght red," my sister and I say when recounting our episodes. Molly not only shares my tendency to turn BRI-ght red, but she has BRI-ght red hair. Moreover, she is gorgeous. Molly has grown up with eyes on her, questions peppering her commute: if not "*You play basketball?*" then, "*Do you model?*" At my sister's six-feet two altitude, there's no place to hide a burst of color.

Self-deprecation she has made her art. Molly has dinner party guests rolling on the floor with first-date catastrophe tales. She digs up photos of herself in fanny packs, visors, braces, and attaches them to group e-mails. I can't tell if this is an entrenched defense mechanism, or if this is a swan, reveling in the ugly duckling days.

Regardless, I've adopted Molly's tactic. I've learned to make fun of my blush before anyone can pity it. To lean on the *BRI* in bright. To mime a facial explosion, using all ten fingers. *Foosh.* Watching Molly lets me imagine that the blush is an element of my charm — sweet, bizarre, old-fashioned, BRI-ight. I try hard to believe that any one inclined to like or love me would like or love me for bleeding emotion through my skin. That the blush is the flourish of an idiosyncratic voice. One that apologizes, but doesn't. That self-loathes as readily as it self-loves. That can't dwell on any gradation of self-perception in between.

"Of course then I turned *BRI-ght* red," I hear myself working into my stories, particularly around people I've recently met. New, uncalibrated audiences. If they think I'm OK with the color storms — or if *I* think *they* think I'm OK — then the flash flood moment is less disarming — to me first, then them, though by them, it doesn't matter. It's my defense mechanism come full circle. I've taken the audience out of the equation. Now: it's a question of charming myself. How convincingly? Can't tell you.

• •

Sister Karen Marie showed us what Christmas looked like, but left it to her Holy Angels pupils to learn about the postcoital blush for themselves.

Before I knew there was such a term, I stood before the wall-to-wall mirror of my dorm room bathroom, one hand raised to one cheek. The cuts of rouge stunned me — how brazenly, how beautifully, the red clashed against the lace-curtain white expanse of chest. Here was a blush in full bloom, no freckle of shame visible beneath it.

    Science claims that the facial coloration of sexual climax has no relation to erythrophobia. What I know science neglects to consider is how much a woman has to let go in order to reach her peak.

• •

In 1990, Shields, Mallory, and Simon discovered a correlation between blushing and age. As subjects grew older, they blushed less — with less *frequency*. No note on the intensity of the facial coloration.

• •

All three sisters are together — Katie, Molly, and I — on vacation, riding in a taxi cab in southern India. Molly lives here now, New Dehli's token six-foot redhead. Just the other day, outside the Taj Mahal, I watched her get mauled by no less than fifty giggle-frenzied school girls and short middle-aged men. "*One snap!*" the strangers chimed, holding up cameras, beckoning family members to join in. The whole crew forsaking the white fortress at our backs. The most photographed site in the world.

    On our taxi ride through the mountains, Molly and I begin exchanging mortifying moments, one-upping each other's crimson climaxes. Molly at Pakistani customs, the intimate contents of her suitcase yanked out. Me: bungling dance lessons in Havana, claiming "*tengo un problema con los pies.*" Molly: fidgeting with PowerPoint, ten quiet coworkers waiting. Me fumbling for my cell phone, a noise-free writer's colony tisking. Stains here, burps there —

    "*God*, you guys," Katie says with disdain. Katie, sitting shotgun, holding her place as oldest child, looks out the cab window. Katie has never been a blusher. She sunburns like an albino, but no rashes of shame. I attribute this to confidence — confidence she grew up *with*, not into. There are no microscopic eyes camping out in Katie's skin.

    "Stop," she commands us. "This is painful."

    We ignore Katie. We keep going. "*Then I turned BRI-ght red . . .*" We pile blush upon blush, until our faces bloom with vicarious shame. "*I'm talking BRI-ght red.*"

    Molly fans her face, the laughter asphyxiating her. "*You DIDN'T . . .*"

    I notice pink blotches at the base of Molly's neck. I've never had neck blotches. Have I?

Katie is shaking her head. Without seeing her face, I know Katie's lips are parted, displeased and uncomprehending. "*Jesus* . . ." she says, wishing her last name was Tomasseli.

I can think of no better use of a reunion of Kinders than this. A mutual roasting, remembering that when I turn the color of Pinot Noir, I'm in beloved company.

I do the honors. Dredge up the latest blush. For old times' sake, I make Katie and Molly squirm and glow, respectively . . .

..

"*I don't like meeting people's eyes so I focus on eyebrows instead.*" I read this admission aloud to a freshman Rhetoric class at the University of Iowa. I'm leaning against the edge of the front desk. It has taken me two and a half months to hazard such a lean, fearing that the fold-up desk would collapse upon meeting the rookie teacher's buttock. Today: so far, so good.

I've just had my students write on a piece of paper:

1) What they find hardest about public speaking

2) What mental trick they use to overcome their fears

Now, after collecting the twenty-three scraps of folded paper, shuffling them for anonymity, I'm sharing with the class.

"*I practice my speech in front of a mirror in my dorm. . . .*"

The University of Iowa requires all freshmen to give three speeches for this Gen-Ed class. The University of Iowa does not give its Rhetoric teaching assistants any guidance on how to teach public speaking. My pedagogy is about as sophisticated as the plastic grin of a soccer mom. I coax; I nod; I'm always the first to clap.

I figure it might behoove them to know that few phobias are unique. And since it's the gimmicks, the mental ploys, the placebos that tide us over until our confidence finds a way to solidify, then I can at least give my students' confessions a safe, faceless forum.

"*I hold my hands in my pockets so no one sees them shake. . . .*"

I interject supportive commentary as I read: "Yup, that's hard for all of us," or "Not a bad idea."

"*I don't think public speaking is that hard so please —*"

My voice slows. It's too late to censor the sentence. I feel twin bull's-eyes emerging on my cheeks. Forty-six silent eyes have me.

"*— stop making such a big deal about it.*"

Rickey Laurentiis

Lord and Chariot

I say the dead done caught me in a special knot
   and lured, and dragged me to the interior.
I say his face is strange here, a moment cruel
   but not without its silk, its earned sadness.
He asks me to touch it, so I touch it. No light
   can blossom here I know, as my bones know.

  • •

Why ask me who I am. Who really knows
   the place of my future? I'm his, or I'm not —
I'm black, or black was made me. The light
   turns the cane a wanted color. I walk its interior.
There are only grasses here, only sadness.
   I pick one. I tear it. I think to be free is to be cruel.

  • •

He says the dead are versions of himself: little ulcers,
   little cruel insurgencies. He says, Know
that I'm master here, my boy, my little sadness.
   There is no riot. (*Riot.*) Or fear. (*Fear.*) Bought, knotted,
I'm the boy in the cane field that's his, the air or
   I'm his whip that stirred the air, scarred the light.

  • •

My back is the touch of violence. Like light,
   my blood trills. I kneel. I ooze. Cruel
underworld, I freeze in your interior —

  Though I'm called queen. I lie at his waist. I know
the true color of his loved-on skin. I say it's white, not
  purity. I say that my strength is my sadness.

  • •

To be free, I think, like him, is a sadness —
  Nothing at all. But to be bold, to light
a panic, to tear a cage of cane by blade is not
  freedom, either. The cane grows back. *Cruel —*
Can't you see it's the one word I know? Even my bones know
  this language, and moan it deep in their interior.

  • •

I say the dead done left me, stranded, at the interior,
  which is this stranger's face, his sprawling sadness.
I say any blade in my hand is just my hand, and I know
  its weight exactly, the lift of its bite. O light:
sweet molestation in the fields. One lord. One chariot. Cruel
  silk, I'm a boy in love. Let the dead, their dead.

109 *Rickey Laurentiis*

Robert Lowell

The Infinite

That hill pushed off by itself was always dear
to me and the hedges near
it that cut away so much of the final horizon.
When I would sit there lost in deliberation,
I reasoned most on the interminable spaces
beyond all hills, on their antediluvian resignation
and silence that passes
beyond man's possibility.
Here for a little while my heart is quiet inside me;
and when the wind lifts roughing through the trees,
I set about comparing my silence to those voices,
and I think about the eternal, the dead seasons,
things here at hand and alive,
and all their reasons and choices.
It's sweet to destroy my mind
and go down
and wreck in this sea where I drown.

Jamaal May

The Sky, Now Black with Birds

Riot helmets outnumbered the protesters
who, after Troy Davis was executed, stuck around
to throw useless punches into the courthouse grass,
while a woman near the forest of batons
lay sprawled facedown in the lawn gripping a Bible,
a green sea beginning to memorize
the shape of her grief. If I say *Death,
cure death*, and have such power over the scythe,
how many cranes will it take to lift her
out of this drowning?
                              If I tell you white
supremacist Lawrence Brewer was executed
five hours earlier for the murder of James Byrd —
if I ask you to look for birds foraging
between his intricate tattoos,
I don't mean to distract you from the cross
that still burned on his arm that day.
I don't expect you to stare into a graffiti
of iron-crosses and spider webs scrawled
across flesh and find a thrush vibrating with birdsong,
but I want you to know why I listen for more
than the cawing of crows:
                            I wanted Brewer dead.
So dead, my tongue swelled fat with hexes, so fat
I wonder how *forgive* could ever fit inside my mouth.
Somehow it's always there, fluttering in the larynx
of Ross Byrd — the man whose father was dragged,
urine soaked, by Lawrence behind a truck.
Watch him say it.

                              Forgive.
I swear,
the word has feathers. I want
to learn to get its wings between my teeth
before more retribution
blots out the sky.
                    When I tell you
glare flickered off a cop's visor
and startled a single crow away
from the murder that flapped the sky into inky pieces,
I want you to watch it close enough
to notice its feathers aren't black at all.
Like bruises and ink, they are
only this full-bodied purple — purple your eyes
will still tell you is black the next time
you see it spread out across sky. Watch it
spread like the flush of pancuronium bromide
into diaphragm, watch close enough to pinpoint
when the muscles lock.
                          If it is said the injection
is humane, we mean to say this
is humanity: no crack of rope, jerk
of limb, no bloated face, clenched jaw, or reek
rising twisted in smoke from a cooked torso —
we mean to say there is nothing to disturb
the nest between our ribs, there is nothing
to make a heartbeat rumble
like a murder of so many wings.

W. S. Merwin

Under the Day

To come back like autumn
to the moss on the stones
after many seasons
to recur as a face
backlit on the surface
of a dark pool one day
after the year has turned
from the summer it saw
while the first yellow leaves
stare from their forgetting
and the branches grow spare

is to waken backward
down through the still water
knowing without touching
all that was ever there
and has been forgotten
and recognize without
name or understanding
without believing or
holding or direction
in the way that we see
at each moment the air.

Philip Metres

The Iraqi Curator's PowerPoint

—for Donny George Youkhanna, 1950-2011, Curator of the Iraq National Museum

You can see the footprints around the hole
The Iraqi Curator said. They smashed the head
Because they could not lift it from its base,
This statue of Nike. It's still missing.
And this is *Umma Al-Ghareb*, my dig site.
The Mother of Scorpions, it means. *Y'anni*,

Next slide: more damage by looters. If the eyes
Are gems, they will be made into holes.
If the skin is gold, goodbye. Now this is a sight:
The bodies too heavy, so they took the heads
Of these terracotta lions. A slide is missing
Here. What I ask you is this: base

What you believe on what you can almost see.
For example: you hear the dogs bay
From the outskirts of the city. They head
Wherever they smell flesh. My eyes
Still see buildings that now are holes.
What you see is not what is missing.

Next slide. I'd heard that Etana, missing
For years, was in Damascus. Then in Beirut.
Then, I got a call from an art friend, a whole
Continent away. Does it have a scratch at the base
Of his hand and along his chest I said he said yes
Of course I said and it is headless

And writing on the shoulder beneath no head
And he said yes and yes the right arm missing
And I said my God I said John take my eyes
And let me see. I was blind and now had sight
Though I could not see it. This is the basis
Of art, *sadiki*. There's something beyond the hole

Which each must face. Missile sites. Army bases.
The hole in the ground where thousands climbed
Into sky. Missing heads of state. Eyes.

Heather Monley
2013 Kenyon Review Short Fiction Contest Winner

Town of Birds

In the town where the children turned into birds, we were not as surprised as you might imagine. Children have always been changing into things — becoming things you wouldn't expect. There was the time the boys grew their hair long so they looked like girls, and the time the girls wore the heavy pants of boys. When the children grew feathers and took to the trees, we believed it was more of the same.

Of course, when the children did not fly home in time for dinner, and then, when the children did not fly home at all, the mothers cried, but mothers have always cried at the things children do.

The children did not change all at once. First were the troublemakers, those smoking behind dumpsters and breaking bottles on empty lots. When large, black birds appeared at these children's houses, waiting at windows and biting at doors, we began to suspect what had happened.

The people in town shook their heads. Kids like that will find any way to shock.

Then more children changed — the good children, the promising. An entire seventh-grade class disappeared. My mother brushed my brother's hair back from his forehead and studied his eyes. He was not much younger than those who had turned.

The birds were not beautiful. They were large, dark and dusky, with long, snaking necks. A breed of cormorant, we learned, was their species.

I was a child, but younger than those who were changing. The older kids had frightened me — their roughness and shouts — and I didn't like them as birds either. When my mother and I walked down by the lake, where the birds had begun to congregate, I eyed the creatures with wide, cool eyes. The birds hunkered dark in the trees and squabbled.

When a child changed into a bird, he retreated from the world. He went to the bathroom or stepped around a corner, and that was the last you saw of him. There never were signs — the change came sudden, or appeared that way. Perhaps for weeks a shift had been occurring deep within the child's body, or perhaps the seed had always been there, spreading outward since birth.

A call came from school — my brother had missed his afternoon classes — and that's how we learned he had changed. That evening, we heard a scraping at the kitchen window, and my mother turned from the stove, her face pink with steam. She opened the window. My brother clambered in, falling to the linoleum, wings pointing out like gangly elbows. He flapped to his usual seat at the table, but when my mother spooned food on his plate, he prodded it with his bill and wouldn't eat. He hopped onto the table and stood in the salad, then lifted up and careened around the house, until we opened the door and he flapped out into the night. He had spoiled our food and broken a candlestick. His guano had stained a seat cushion.

He didn't enter the house again. My mother scavenged food for him — fish, crustaceans, certain insects — and brought these to the windowsill, where my brother swallowed them whole, still living. My mother reached her fingers toward his wings, but my brother skittered away. Soon, he wouldn't come to the window but waited for his supper on the front lawn, jutting his head forward and back. My mother stood in the yard and threw fish, still alive and flipping. All over town, mothers threw fish to beckon the children.

My brother stopped coming to the house at all. He was lost to the trees and lake.

We walked down to the water, where the birds grunted and dove, and tried to pick out my brother from the others. That one, my mother said, pointing to a bird on a rock, wings stretched out to dry the feathers. She straightened her jaw. It has to be that one. I think.

As the months passed, the birds' feathers changed — from the dull, dusky tone of youths, to a mature and inky black. In the summer, they gathered sticks and lake grass and flotsam, and built nests high in the trees. We watched the nests through binoculars. Soon, above the twigs, small feeble things poked their heads — the grandchildren of the town.

The children kept changing. As the young in our town reached a certain age, they flapped off to the lake. As the years passed, it became a matter of course, and when a boy's chin grew a few strands of hair, or a girl came to laugh in a certain way, the old people said, It can't be long now.

A few children remained human, and we'd see them, these teenagers, walking to their empty classes, silent and pale. We younger children, we didn't wish to become ones like these. We prepared for an avian life.

We ran wild. Why teach them manners? our mothers said. They'll be birds soon enough. We ran through the streets and down to the lake, watching the birds dive and emerge with fish. We sat at the lakeshore and threw rocks into the water, perhaps in the birds' direction, but we would not throw rocks at the birds themselves. We were too afraid.

Soon I'd reached the proper age, and my companions started changing. Once, we caught a boy sneaking from class and pursued him onto the playing field. He stopped, his back to us, and wrapped his arms around himself. He seemed to be wearing a dark cape, but as we approached, the cape became feathers, and he spread them out into wings. He lifted from the ground and flew to the trees that bordered the school, and there we could not catch him.

One by one, they disappeared. I skipped school, went hiding, climbed trees, waiting for something to overcome me. When children younger than I started changing, I knew I'd been left behind.

A town so blighted cannot last long. Our children had not grown into adults, and no one was left to run the businesses. Main street windows boarded up. Families gathered their things and moved away. The others like me, who had not changed — they left as soon as they could.

But my mother and I stay on — we seem unable to leave. She watches the cormorants fly low over the yard, their necks outstretched, wings swimming through air. She speaks of my brother. Always the best of sons, she says. He wanted to be a doctor.

Often I walk down to the lake and sit at the shore, where our silent town is still cacophonous. The birds' numbers grow. The trees around the lake stink with their feces, and the guano has killed off the underbrush.

I watch the birds on the rocks, in the trees, in the water. I strip off my clothes and stand before them. Their eyes are like jewels. I dive into the lake and imagine the water pulls back my skin, revealing something new and black underneath. I want the birds to take me away.

So many places come to their end. Our town is no different from any of them.

Marianne Moore

A Glass-Ribbed Nest

    For authorities whose hopes
are shaped by mercenaries?
    Writers entrapped by
    teatime fame and by
commuters' comforts? Not for these
    the paper nautilus
constructs her thin glass shell.

    Giving her perishable
souvenir of hope, a dull
    white outside and smooth-
    edged inner side as
glossy as the sea, the watchful
    animal takes charge of
    it herself and scarcely

    leaves it till the eggs are hatched.
Buried eight-fold in her eight
    arms, for she is in
    a sense a devil-
fish, her glass ramshorn-cradled freight
    is hid but is not crushed.
    As Hercules, bitten

    by a crab loyal to the hydra,
was hindered to succeed,
    the intensively
    watched eggs coming from
the shell, free it when they are freed, —
    leaving its wasp-nest flaws
    of white on white, and close-

laid Ionic chiton-folds
like the lines in the mane of
    a Parthenon horse,
    round which the arms had
wound themselves as if they knew love
    is the only fortress
    strong enough to trust to.

Diana Khoi Nguyen

Getting the Hero to Speak

This is the hardest part:
    when they touch me
under the frenzy of those who love
    They dab their hair in oil
    Black flies cling to their lips.

digging beneath the broomrape
like a severed root of aloe

    sometimes wine & milk
        They pour blood
    bending low
from the stalk of a wort
        its serration.
    in their saucers.
        Once
a virgin leaned over the small portal
        from her fork—
            like a canary.
to make room for those that bite best.

the paralysis required
    my heart clapping like swans
& those who shine.
then force it into my mouth.

In bloodied tunics they sing
& rampion where I keep
    a tube to my mouth.
Sometimes they pour honey
or water.
    when they want me to speak
        like a tendril once stripped
a fiddlehead uncranking
    The ram hearts cool gently

egg yolk dripping
    it filled my tomb
Teeth fall out

Flannery O'Connor

The Life You Save May Be Your Own

The old woman and her daughter were sitting on their porch when Mr. Shiftlet came up their road for the first time. The old woman slid to the edge of her chair and leaned forward, shading her eyes from the piercing sunset with her hand. The daughter could not see far in front of her and continued to play with her fingers. Although the old woman lived in this desolate spot with only her daughter and she had never seen Mr. Shiftlet before, she could tell, even from a distance, that he was a tramp and no one to be afraid of. His left coat sleeve was folded up to show there was only half an arm in it and his gaunt figure listed slightly to the side as if the breeze were pushing him. He had on a black town suit and a brown felt hat that was turned up in the front and down in the back and he carried a tin tool box by a handle. He came on, at an amble, up her road, his face turned toward the sun which appeared to be balancing itself on the peak of a small mountain.

The old woman didn't change her position until he was almost into her yard; then she rose with one hand fisted on her hip. The daughter, a large girl in a short blue organdy dress, saw him all at once and jumped up and began to stamp and point and make excited speechless sounds.

Mr. Shiftlet stopped just inside the yard and set his box on the ground and tipped his hat at her as if she were not in the least afflicted; then he turned toward the old woman and swung the hat all the way off. He had long black slick hair that hung flat from a part in the middle to beyond the tips of his ears on either side. His face descended in forehead for more than half its length and ended suddenly with his features just balanced over a jutting steel-trap jaw. He seemed to be a young man but he had a look of composed dissatisfaction as if he understood life thoroughly.

"Good evening," the old woman said. She was about the size of a cedar fence post and she had a man's grey hat pulled down low over her head.

The tramp stood looking at her and didn't answer. He turned his back and faced the sunset. He swung both his whole and his short arm up slowly so that they indicated an expanse of sky and his figure formed a crooked cross. The old woman watched him with her arms folded across her chest as if she were the owner of the sun, and the daughter watched, her head thrust forward and her fat helpless hands hanging at the wrists. She had long pink-gold hair and eyes as blue as a peacock's neck.

He held the pose for almost fifty seconds and then he picked up his box and came on to the porch and dropped down on the bottom step. "Lady," he said in a firm nasal voice, "I'd give a fortune to live where I could see me a sun do that every evening."

"Does it every evening," the old woman said and sat back down. The daughter sat down too and watched him with a cautious sly look as if he were a bird that had come up very close. He leaned to one side, rooting in his pants pocket, and in a second he brought out a package of chewing gum and offered her a piece. She took it and unpeeled it and began to chew without taking her eyes off him. He offered the old woman a piece but she only raised her upper lip to indicate she had no teeth.

Mr. Shiftlet's pale sharp glance had already passed over everything in the yard — the pump near the corner of the house and the big fig tree that three or four chickens were preparing to roost in — and had moved to a shed where he saw the square rusted back of an automobile. "You ladies drive?" he asked.

"That car ain't run in fifteen year," the old woman said. "The day my husband died, it quit running."

"Nothing is like it used to be, Lady," he said. "The world is almost rotten."

"That's right," the old woman said. "You from around here?"

"Name Tom T. Shiftlet," he murmured, looking at the tires.

"I'm pleased to meet you," the old woman said. "Name Lucynell Crater and daughter Lucynell Crater. What you doing around here, Mr. Shiftlet?"

He judged the car to be about a 1928 or '29 Ford. "Lady," he said, and turned and gave her his full attention, "lemme tell you something. There's one of these doctors in Atlanta that's taken a knife and cut the human heart — the human heart," he repeated, leaning forward, "out of a man's chest and held it in his hand," and he held his hand out, palm up, as if it were slightly weighted with the human heart, "and studied it like it was a day-old chicken, and Lady," he said, allowing a long significant pause in which his head slid forward and his clay-colored eyes brightened, "he don't know no more about it than you or me."

"That's right," the old woman said.

"Why, if he was to take that knife and cut into every corner of it, he still wouldn't know no more than you or me. What you want to bet?"

"Nothing," the old woman said wisely. "Where you come from, Mr. Shiftlet?"

He didn't answer. He reached into his pocket and brought out a sack of tobacco and a package of cigarette papers and rolled himself a cigarette, expertly with one hand, and attached it in a hanging position to his upper lip. Then he took a box of wooden matches from his pocket and struck one on his shoe. He held the burning match as if he were studying the mystery of flame while it traveled dangerously toward his skin. The daughter began to make loud noises and to point to his hand and shake her finger at him, but when the flame was just before touching him, he leaned down with his hand cupped over it as if he were going to set fire to his nose and lit the cigarette.

He flipped away the dead match and blew a stream of grey into the evening. A sly look came over his face. "Lady," he said, "nowadays, people'll do anything anyways. I can tell you my name is Tom T. Shiftlet and I come from Tarwater, Tennessee, but you never have seen me before: how you know I ain't lying? How you know my name ain't Aaron Sparks, Lady, and I come from Singleberry, Georgia, or how you know it's not George Speeds and I come from Lucy, Alabama, or how you know I ain't Thompson Bright from Toolafalls, Mississippi?"

"I don't know nothing about you," the old woman muttered, irked.

"Lady," he said, "people don't care how they lie. Maybe the best I can tell you is, I'm a man, but listen, Lady," he said and paused and made his tone more ominous still, "what is a man?"

The old woman began to gum a seed. "What you carry in that tin box, Mr. Shiftlet?" she asked.

"Tools," he said, put back. "I'm a carpenter."

"Well, if you come out here to work, I'll be able to feed you and give you a place to sleep but I can't pay. I'll tell you that before you begin," she said.

There was no answer at once and no particular expression on his face. He leaned back against the two-by-four that helped support the porch roof. "Lady," he said slowly, "there's some men that some things mean more to them than money." The old woman rocked without comment and the daughter watched the trigger that moved up and down in his neck. He told the old woman then that all most people were interested in was money, but he asked what a man was made for. He asked her if a man was made for money, or what. He asked her what she thought she was made for but she didn't answer, she only sat rocking and wondered if a one-armed man could put a new roof on her garden house. He asked a lot of questions that she didn't answer. He told her that he was twenty-eight years old and had lived a varied life. He had been a gospel singer, a foreman on the railroad, an assistant in an undertaking parlor, and he had come over the radio for three months with Uncle Roy and his Red Creek Wranglers. He said he had fought and bled in the Arm Service of his country and visited every foreign land and that everywhere he had seen people that didn't care if they did a thing one way or another. He said he hadn't been raised thataway.

A fat yellow moon appeared in the branches of the fig tree as if it were going to roost there with the chickens. He said that a man had to escape to the country to see the world whole and that he wished he lived in a desolate place like this where he could see the sun go down every evening like God made it to do.

"Are you married or are you single?" the old woman asked.

There was a long silence. "Lady," he asked finally, "where would you find you an innocent woman today? I wouldn't have any of this trash I could just pick up."

The daughter was leaning very far down, hanging her head almost between her knees, watching him through a triangular door she had made in her overturned hair; and she suddenly fell in a heap on the floor and began to whimper. Mr. Shiftlet straightened her out and helped her get back in the chair.

"Is she your baby girl?" he asked.

"My only," the old woman said, "and she's the sweetest girl in the world. I wouldn't give her up for nothing on earth. She's smart too. She can sweep the floor, cook, wash, feed the chickens, and hoe. I wouldn't give her up for a casket of jewels."

"No," he said kindly, "don't ever let any man take her away from you."

"Any man come after her," the old woman said, " 'll have to stay around the place."

Mr. Shiftlet's eye in the darkness was focussed on a part of the automobile bumper that glittered in the distance. "Lady," he said, jerking his short arm up as if he could point with it to her house and yard and pump, "there ain't a broken thing on this plantation that I couldn't fix for you, one-arm jackleg or not. I'm a man," he said with a sullen dignity, "even if I ain't a whole one. I got," he said, tapping his knuckles on the floor to emphasize the immensity of what he was going to say, "a moral intelligence!" and his face pierced out of the darkness into a shaft of doorlight and he stared at her as if he were astonished himself at this impossible truth.

The old woman was not impressed with the phrase. "I told you you could hang around and work for food," she said, "if you don't mind sleeping in that car yonder."

"Why listen, Lady," he said with a grin of delight, "the monks of old slept in their coffins!"

"They wasn't as advanced as we are," the old woman said.

The next morning he began on the roof of the garden house while Lucynell, the daughter, sat on a rock and watched him work. He had not been around a week before the change he had made in the place was apparent. He had patched the front and back steps, built a new hog pen, restored a fence, and taught Lucynell who was completely deaf, and had never said a word in her life, to say the word "bird." The big rosy-faced girl followed him everywhere, saying "Burrttddt ddbirrrttdt," and clapping her hands. The old woman watched from a distance, secretly pleased. She was ravenous for a son-in-law.

Mr. Shiftlet slept on the hard narrow back seat of the car with his feet out the side window. He had his razor and a can of water on a crate that served him as a bedside table and he put up a piece of mirror against the back glass and kept his coat neatly on a hanger that he hung over one of the windows.

In the evenings he sat on the steps and talked while the old woman and Lucynell rocked violently in their chairs on either side of him. The old woman's three mountains were black against the dark blue sky and were visited off and on by various planets and by the moon after it had left the chickens. Mr. Shiftlet pointed out that the reason he had improved this plantation was because he had taken a personal interest in it. He said he was even going to make the automobile run.

He had raised the hood and studied the mechanism and he said he could tell that the car had been built in the days when cars were really built. You take now, he said, one man puts in one bolt and another man puts in another bolt and another man puts in another bolt so that it's a man for a bolt. That's why you have to pay so much for a car: you're paying all those men. Now if you didn't have to pay but one man, you could get you a cheaper car and one that had had a personal interest taken in it, and it would be a better car. The old woman agreed with him that this was so.

Mr. Shiftlet said that the trouble with the world was that nobody cared, or stopped and took any trouble. He said he never would have been able to teach Lucynell to say a word if he hadn't cared and stopped long enough.

"Teach her to say something else," the old woman said.

"What you want her to say next?" Mr. Shiftlet asked.

The old woman's smile was broad and toothless and suggestive. "Teach her to say 'sugarpie,'" she said.

Mr. Shiftlet already knew what was on her mind.

The next day he began to tinker with the automobile and that evening he told her that if she would buy a fan belt, he would be able to make the car run.

The old woman said she would give him the money. "You see that girl yonder?" she asked, pointing to Lucynell who was sitting on the floor a foot away, watching him, her eyes blue even in the dark. "If it was ever a man wanted to take her away, I would say, 'No man on earth is going to take that sweet girl of mine away from me!' but if he was to say, 'Lady, I don't want to take her away, I want her right here,' I would say, 'Mister, I don't blame you none. I wouldn't pass up a chance to live in a permanent place and get the sweetest girl in the world myself. You ain't no fool,' I would say."

"How old is she?" Mr. Shiftlet asked casually.

"Fifteen, sixteen," the old woman said. The girl was nearly thirty but because of her innocence it was impossible to guess.

"It would be a good idea to paint it too," Mr. Shiftlet remarked. "You don't want it to rust out."

"We'll see about that later," the old woman said.

The next day he walked into town and returned with the parts he needed and a can of gasoline. Late in the afternoon, terrible noises issued from the shed and the old woman rushed out of the house, thinking Lucynell was somewhere having a fit. Lucynell was sitting on a chicken crate, stamping her feet and screaming, "Burrddttt! bddurrd-dttt!" but her fuss was drowned out by the car. With a volley of blasts it emerged from the shed, moving in a fierce and stately way. Mr. Shiftlet was in the driver's seat, sitting very erect. He had an expression of serious modesty on his face as if he had just raised the dead.

That night, rocking on the porch, the old woman began her business at once. "You want you an innocent woman, don't you?" she asked sympathetically. "You don't want none of this trash."

"No'm, I don't," Mr. Shiftlet said.

"One that can't talk," she continued, "can't sass you back or use foul language. That's the kind for you to have. Right there," and she pointed to Lucynell sitting cross-legged in her chair, holding both feet in her hands.

"That's right," he admitted. "She wouldn't give me any trouble."

"Saturday," the old woman said, "you and her and me can drive into town and get married."

Mr. Shiftlet eased his position on the steps.

"I can't get married right now," he said. "Everything you want to do takes money and I ain't got any."

"What you need with money?" she asked.

"It takes money," he said. "Some people'll do anything any how these days, but the way I think, I wouldn't marry no woman that I couldn't take on a trip like she was somebody. I mean take her to a hotel and treat her. I wouldn't marry the Duchesser Windsor," he said firmly, "unless I could take her to a hotel and give her something good to eat.

"I was raised thataway and there ain't a thing I can do about it. My old mother taught me how to do."

"Lucynell don't even know what a hotel is," the old woman muttered. "Listen here, Mr. Shiftlet," she said sliding forward in her chair, "you'd be getting a permanent house and a deep well and the most innocent girl in the world. You don't need no money. Lemme tell you something: there ain't any place in the world for a poor disabled friendless drifting man."

The ugly words settled in Mr. Shiftlet's head like a group or buzzards in the top of a tree. He didn't answer at once. He rolled himself a cigarette and lit it and then he said in an even voice, "Lady, a man is divided into two parts, body and spirit."

The old woman clamped her gums together.

"A body and a spirit," he repeated. "The body, Lady, is like a house: it don't go anywhere; but the spirit, Lady, is like a automobile: always on the move, always. . . . "

"Listen, Mr. Shiftlet," she said, "my well never goes dry and my house is always warm in the winter and there's no mortgage on a thing about this place. You can go to the court house and see for yourself. And yonder under that shed is a fine automobile." She laid the bait carefully. "You can have it painted by Saturday. I'll pay for the paint."

In the darkness, Mr. Shiftlet's smile stretched like a weary snake waking up by a fire. "Yes'm," he said softly.

After a second he recalled himself and said, "I'm only saying a man's spirit means more to him than anything else. I would have to take my wife off for the weekend without no regards at all for cost. I got to follow where my spirit says to go."

"I'll give you fifteen dollars for a weekend trip," the old woman said in a crabbed voice. "That's the best I can do."

"That wouldn't hardly pay for more than the gas and the hotel," he said. "It wouldn't feed her."

"Seventeen-fifty," the old woman said. "That's all I got so it isn't any use you trying to milk me. You can take a lunch."

Mr. Shiftlet was deeply hurt by the word "milk." He didn't doubt that she had more money sewed up in her mattress but he had already told her he was not interested in her money. "I'll make that do," he said and rose and walked off without treating with her further.

On Saturday the three of them drove into town in the car that the paint had barely dried on and Mr. Shiftlet and Lucynell were married in the Ordinary's office while the old woman witnessed. As they came out of the courthouse, Mr. Shiftlet began twisting his neck in his collar. He looked morose and bitter as if he had been insulted while some one held him. "That didn't satisfy me none," he said. "That was just something a woman in an office did, nothing but paper work and blood tests. What do they know about my blood? If they was to take my heart and cut it out," he said, "they wouldn't know a thing about me. It didn't satisfy me at all."

"It satisfied the law," the old woman said sharply.

"The law," Mr. Shiftlet said and spit. "It's the law that don't satisfy me."

He had painted the car dark green with a yellow band around it just under the windows. The three of them climbed in the front seat and the old woman said, "Don't Lucynell look pretty? Looks like a baby doll." Lucynell was dressed up in a white dress that her mother had uprooted from a trunk and there was a panama hat on her head with a bunch of red wooden cherries on the brim. Every now and then her placid expression was changed by a sly isolated little thought like a shoot of green in the desert. "You got a prize!" the old woman said.

Mr. Shiftlet didn't even look at her.

They drove back to the house to let the old woman off and pick up the lunch. When they were ready to leave, she stood staring in the window of the car, with her fingers clenched around the glass. Tears began to seep sideways out of her eyes and run along the dirty creases in her face. "I ain't ever been parted with her for two days before," she said.

Mr. Shiftlet started the motor.

"And I wouldn't let no man have her but you because I seen you would do right. Goodbye, Sugarbaby," she said, clutching at the sleeve of the white dress. Lucynell looked straight at her and didn't seem to see her there at all. Mr. Shiftlet eased the car forward so that she had to move her hands.

The early afternoon was clear and open and surrounded by pale blue sky. The hills flattened under the car one after another and the climb and dip and swerve went entirely to Mr. Shiftlet's head so that he forgot his morning bitterness. He had always wanted an automobile but he had never been able to afford one before. He drove very fast because he wanted to make Mobile by nightfall.

Occasionally he stopped his thoughts long enough to look at Lucynell in the seat beside him. She had eaten the lunch as soon as they were out of the yard and now she was pulling the cherries off the hat one by one and throwing them out the window. He became depressed in spite of the car. He had driven about a hundred miles when he decided that she must be hungry again and at the next small town they came to, he stopped in front of an aluminum-painted eating place called The Hot Spot and took her in and ordered her a plate of ham and grits. The ride had made her sleepy and as soon as she got up on the stool, she rested her head on the counter and shut her eyes. There was no one in the Hot Spot but Mr. Shiftlet and the boy behind the counter, a pale youth with a greasy rag hung over his shoulder. Before he could dish up the food, she was snoring gently.

"Give it to her when she wakes up," Mr. Shiftlet said. "I'll pay for it now."

The boy bent over her and stared at the long pink-gold hair and the half-shut sleeping eyes. Then he looked up and stared at Mr. Shiftlet. "She looks like an angel of Gawd," he murmured.

"Hitch-hiker," Mr. Shiftlet explained. "I can't wait. I got to make Tuscaloosa."

The boy bent over again and very carefully touched his finger to a strand of the golden hair and Mr. Shiftlet left.

He was more depressed than ever as he drove on by himself. The late afternoon had grown hot and sultry and the country had flattened out. Deep in the sky a storm was preparing very slowly and without thunder as if it meant to drain every drop of air from the earth before it broke. There were times when Mr. Shiftlet preferred not to be alone. He felt too that a man with a car had a responsibility to others and he kept his eye out for a hitchhiker. Occasionally he saw a sign that warned: "Drive carefully. The life you save may be your own."

The narrow road dropped off on either side into dry fields and here and there a shack or a filling station stood in a clearing. The sun began to set directly in front of the automobile. It was a reddening ball that through his windshield was slightly flat on the bottom and top. He saw a boy in overalls and a grey hat, standing on the edge of the road and he slowed the car down and stopped in front of him. The boy didn't have his hand raised to thumb the ride, he was only standing there, but he had a small cardboard suitcase and his hat was set on his head in a way to indicate that he had left somewhere for good. "Son," Mr. Shiftlet said, "I see you want a ride."

The boy didn't say he did or he didn't but he opened the door of the car and got in, and Mr. Shiftlet started driving again. The child held the suitcase on his lap and folded his arms on top of it. He turned his head and looked out the window away from Mr. Shiftlet. Mr. Shiftlet felt oppressed. "Son," he said after a minute, "I got the best old mother in the world so I reckon you only got the second best."

The boy gave him a quick dark glance and then turned his face back out the window.

"It's nothing so sweet," Mr. Shiftlet continued, "as a boy's mother. She taught him his first prayers at her knee, she give him love when no other would, she told him what was right and what wasn't, and she seen that he done the right thing. Son," he said, "I never rued a day in my life like the one I rued when I left that old mother of mine."

The boy shifted in his seat but he didn't look at Mr. Shiftlet. He unfolded his arms and put one hand on the door handle.

"My mother was a angel of Gawd," Mr. Shiftlet said in a very strained voice. "He took her from heaven and giver to me and I left her." His eyes were instantly clouded over with a mist of tears.

The boy turned angrily in the seat. "You go to the devil!" he cried. "My old woman is a flea bag and your's is a stinking pole cat!" and with that he flung the door open and jumped out with his suitcase into the ditch.

Mr. Shiftlet was so shocked that for about a hundred feet he drove along slowly with the door still open like his mouth. Then he reached over and shut both. A cloud, the exact color of the boy's hat and shaped like a turnip, had descended over the sun, and another, worse looking, crouched behind the car. Mr. Shiftlet felt that the rottenness of the world was about to engulf him. He raised his arm and let it fall again to his breast. "Oh Lord!" he prayed, "break forth and wash the slime from this earth!"

The turnip continued slowly to descend. After a few minutes there was a guffawing peal of thunder from behind and fantastic raindrops, like tin can tops, crashed over the rear of Mr. Shiftlet's car. Very quickly he pushed in his clutch and stepped on the gas and, with his stump sticking out the window, he raced the galloping shower into Mobile.

Matthew Olzmann

In the Gallery of American Violence

the musket sulks in the corner.
Not only is it exhausted, it feels
utterly humiliated. A pack of wild
school kids huddles around
the display case, bored,
terribly skeptical that this device —
with its smoothbore barrel
and cherrywood stock — could have ever
punched a hole in a bewildered soldier.
They scribble a few notes then dash off
to some flashier exhibit:
an early landmine perhaps,
or a car window used in a modern drive-by.
How lonely the musket feels, forgotten
in its glass prison, dust on its muzzle,
dust in its mouth. Send me back to the end
of the eighteenth century, it thinks.
There, it stalked the battlefields,
a god without mercy. Blood on the blades
of grass, blood on its bayonet,
a hungry tooth. A celebration
thunder-stomping its way through the smoke.
Cannon songs. Banners waving in the dark.
There were fewer stars, it thinks, on the flag
back then, but more in the sky.

Lucia Perillo

Wild Birds Unlimited

Because the old feeder feeds nothing
but squirrels, who are crafty and have learned
how to hang so it swings sideways until
gravity takes the seed — I bumble down

to this store of bird knick-knacks and
lensware for the geeks, and while
the clerk is ringing up my Mini
Bandit Buster ($29.95), spring-loaded

to close the seed-holes when a heavy animal alights,
I read a pamphlet about bird-feeding, which I had not thought
was complicated, but turns out
is. Yes I bought the costly mixture,

not the cheap stuff, full of milo,
which the birds kick to the ground, where it becomes
an aggregate of shit and chaff.
But I'd not known you must sweep it up

so as not to spread the pathogens, and space
your feeders far apart and dump
the seed each week and clean the feeder tube with bleach.
And you should white-wash the windows of your home

so the birds won't crash — you'll live in twilight
but your conscience will be clear. Otherwise
it's best not to feed the birds
at all: your help will only kill them, has killed them,

I killed them says Wild Birds Unlimited — thanks,
now let me tell you that your wind chimes

turn this place into a gong-tormented sea.
Outside, it's just another shop in the strip mall;

used to be that this place was a grove
of cedars where I knelt in the purplebrown duff
while something holy landed like a lunar rover
on my shoulder. But listen

to what sings in the grove's bright stead—
computer chips provide what you would hear here
if they weren't— mechanical birds
on plastic boughs, always flowering.

Carl Phillips

Radiance Versus Ordinary Light

Meanwhile the sea moves uneasily, like a man who
suspects what the room reels with as he rises into it
is violation — his own: he touches the bruises at each
shoulder and, on his chest,
        the larger bruise, star-shaped,
a flawed star, or hand, though he remembers no hands,
has tried — can't remember . . .
          That kind of rhythm to it,
even to the roughest surf there's a rhythm findable,
which is why we keep coming here, to find it, or that's
what we say. We dive in and, as usual,
         the swimming
feels like that swimming the mind does in the wake
of transgression, how the instinct to panic at first
slackens that much more quickly, if you don't
look back. Regret,
     like pity, changes nothing really, we
say to ourselves and, less often, to each other, each time
swimming a bit farther,
        leaving the shore the way
the water — in its own watered, of course, version
of semaphore — keeps leaving the subject out, flashing
Why should it matter now, and *Why*,
          why shouldn't it,
as the waves beat harder, hard against us, until that's
how we like it, I'll break your heart, break mine.

Sylvia Plath

The Beekeeper's Daughter

A garden of mouthings. Purple, scarlet-speckled, black
The great corollas dilate, peeling back their silks.
Their musk encroaches, circle after circle,
A well of scents almost too dense to breathe in.
Hieratical in your frock coat, maestro of the bees,
You move among the many-breasted hives,

My heart under your foot, sister of a stone.

Trumpet-throats open to the beaks of birds.
The Golden Rain Tree drips its powders down.
In these little boudoirs streaked with orange and red
The anthers nod their heads, potent as kings
To father dynasties. The air is rich.
Here is a queenship no mother can contest —

A fruit that's death to taste: dark flesh, dark parings.

In burrows narrow as a finger, solitary bees
Keep house among the grasses. Kneeling down
I set my eye to a hole-mouth and meet an eye
Round, green, disconsolate as a tear.
Father, bridegroom, in this Easter egg
Under the coronal of sugar roses

The queen bee marries the winter of your year.

D. A. Powell

Calling All Gods

Because I stand with my great unknowing yap and pray for speech.
Because I would open my body like a rasping bellows and have you fill it.
I do not know your name.
That's the zigzag lightning I know.
And that's the stout oak taken down by wind.
But what else am I to call you when you take me up in your embrace.
You've always touched me with a stranger's hand.

What is language outside the body but dry echo, the reflected want.
I stood on the embankment where the midges fussed about the water.
The black wings took them.
The dark celebration overtook its congeries.
No other voices but the frogs. No other sermon but the swallow's call.
Why did you not enter me there with all the others.
Oh, didn't you just. Oh, didn't you give and thrust.
But spoke no word.

No one man can be all things. That's why we need the river's indecisive swell.
I, of course.
I wait for you, the evening.
Abandoned boathouse hallelujah.
I have come to speech. I have turned to kiss your face.
I find your face in every corner of the congregated night.
And I am filled with tongues.

John Crowe Ransom

Winter Remembered

Two evils, monstrous either one apart,
Possessed me, and were long and loath at going:
A cry of Absence, Absence, in the heart,
And in the wood the furious winter blowing.

Think not, when fire was bright upon my bricks,
And past the tight boards hardly a wind could enter,
I glowed like them, the simple burning sticks,
Far from my cause, my proper heat and center.

Better to walk forth in the frozen air
And wash my wound in the snows; that would be healing;
Because my heart would throb less painful there,
Being caked with cold, and past the smart of feeling.

And where I walked, the murderous winter blast
Would have this body bowed, these eyeballs streaming,
And though I think this heart's blood froze not fast
It ran too small to spare one drop for dreaming.

Dear love, these fingers that had known your touch,
And tied our separate forces first together,
Were ten poor idiot fingers not worth much,
Ten frozen parsnips hanging in the weather.

Theodore Roethke

A Light Breather

The spirit moves,
Yet stays:
Stirs as a blossom stirs,
Still wet from its bud-sheath,
Slowly unfolding,
Turning in the light with its tendrils;
Plays as a minnow plays,
Tethered to a limp weed, swinging,
Tail around, nosing in and out of the current,
Its shadow loose, a watery finger;
Moves, like the snail,
Still and inward,
Taking and embracing its surroundings,
Never wishing itself away,
Unafraid of what it is,
A music in a hood,
A small thing,
Singing.

Onnesha Roychoudhuri

Where I'm Writing From

Aw-nay-shuh: the jaw hinging open, letting loose the tongue that flicks across the top of the palate, before retreating behind the teeth to nestle into its postalveolar hush. Aw. Nay. Shuh. Or, rather, Onnesha, in its proper spelling. It wasn't until I was thirty that I thought to give restaurants a simpler name to hold a reservation. I still pause and feel guilty every time I say, "Anna." Like somehow I'm trying to pass. I expect this person who doesn't give a shit to look at me, say, "There's no way your name is Anna."

During a brief phase when I was six or seven, I requested that my family refer to me as Elizabeth. My mother asked me didn't I like my own name, which was much more unique and beautiful? It was a solid parenting gesture, though confusing as it was coming from a woman named Pamela with long, straight, blondish brown locks and blue eyes. There was power in a name, and I figured if mine were Elizabeth, maybe the blue eyes and blonde hair would follow. I would look more like her. My mother. She has stories of walking around — me in her arms, my brother in a stroller — and people asking what country we were adopted from. My mother is too polite to say things like, *The country of my vagina.*

In elementary school, on the first day of class or whenever there was a substitute, I knew when to raise my hand and say "here." It was that pause. A person wondering if they had the necessary gear to scale the heap of consonants and vowels that compose my name. *Here.* It was a kind of preemptive strike — to be in on the joke before it could be made. Like: *I already know what you're thinking. I get it. My name is ridiculous.*

..

"Onnesha" is a name that means, in its more positive connotations, "playful" or "joyful and spritely." Its dark side, its shadow-self, is something wilier: think "trickster" or "bastard." Go ahead. Think it.

. .

I was in grad school before I realized maybe I had more of an issue with names. Every writer has it a little bit: *Should this character be named Susan or Margaret?* But I would just sit there, not able to write a word on the page because, well, if she's named "Ananda," will people assume she's 100 percent Indian? In which case, what is a 100 percent Indian like? Or, maybe she's named Ananda, but she's like me and she's only half Indian, but then the story feels like it has to be about *that* when I just want to follow this character wherever she wants to take me — to bars and on hikes in the woods and sobbing into her ramen. I could name the character Mary, but then will people assume she's a white American? Or maybe she's named Mary, but she's a quarter black and also Italian . . .

In my graduate thesis advisor's office, I tried to articulate the name hang-up. *Just pick a name*, N. said. *You can always change it later*. I explained the treacherous stakes. The way the name could change the course of what might happen, of what's possible. But she just got that look on her face that conveyed a sentiment I know all too well now that I have my own students: *Please stop making me go inside your head. It is exhausting enough to be in my own head and they do not pay me nearly enough money for this.*

Of course I looked to other writers. To figure out where I fit in. In high school, I discovered Salman Rushdie, Chitra Divakaruni, Jhumpa Lahiri. I studied them, not only because I loved the way they told stories, but because I thought I'd be able to understand who I was. Maybe what animated them was what animated me. After Lahiri's novel *Unaccustomed Earth* came out, a reviewer for *Entertainment Weekly* wrote, "Would Jhumpa Lahiri's fiction still work if the Rahuls and Chitras were Roberts and Charlottes? If the mango-lime pickle on the refrigerator shelf were Best Foods mayonnaise?"

The reviewer goes on to encourage us to "strip away the exotic trappings" so that we can see that "her urban professionals could be any anxious, overachieving Americans adrift from their cultural moorings."

Wash off the brown and these characters could totally be Americans, by which I mean white! This seemed like a deeply offensive way to read her fiction until I noticed that one of Lahiri's own stories features a white American narrator who fixates on his roommate's "dark red-hot lime pickle" which "lived next to his peanut butter in the door of the refrigerator."

And now that I was thinking about it: Lahiri's narratives were full of Indian characters that date or marry "Americans," which always seems to operate as a code word for "white." Amit is married to a successful "American" doctor. When he looks at his children, Maya and Monika, he notices they "inherited Megan's coloring, without a trace of [his] deeply tan skin and black eyes, so that apart from their vaguely Indian names they appeared fully American." *American* like his wife who is tall, attractive, and has lighter skin. It is a world in which there are only two kinds of people: Indians and white people.

In the small town in Connecticut where I grew up, there was a church and all the Christians who went there were white. Well, that's not true. What I mean is that almost all of the people in the town were white. And I would sometimes go to church with my mother because I liked the smell of the dusty sanctum, how after the sermon, normally taciturn folks asked after each other's families and offered to bring over casseroles. It was like a scene out of a Laura Ingalls Wilder book, and I'd return home wanting to call my father "Pa" instead of "Baba." I imagined that this is what baptism might be — to be washed clean. White. They had been returned to some neutral state that allowed them to think of other things — whatever they wanted. Mary. Bob. You could be anyone.

As a kid, I didn't really understand that "alien" had more than one definition. I knew my father — Chandrasekhar — was an alien, but he was an alien in both senses of the word. The way Alf was. Alf came from another planet and ate cats, but the show was really about a family that has a secret. A secret that must remain so, presumably because no one else would understand Alf's alien ways. They had to protect him because they had to protect themselves: they were harboring an alien. My dad enjoyed this kind of entertainment — "Alf," "Perfect Strangers," "Gilligan's Island," "Herbie the Love Bug." Shows where the world was skewed, where being an outsider leads to hijinks and laugh tracks.

I can't watch shows that have laugh tracks anymore. I spent my childhood being given cues for when to laugh — and I obeyed. Now I'm like a well-trained dog that recognizes a command but only wants to bite.

..

> I am an English man, and naked I stand here,
> Musyng in my mynde what raiment I shal were;
> For now I wull were thys, and now I wyl were that;

In 1542, a book was published in what is now called Britain. The kind of book that would today be called a coffee table book. This was a long time ago and there were different names or no names at all for certain things. The book was Boorde's illustrated guide to people, featuring a photo of a white male in the nude, armed with a pair of scissors. These, the author notes, were for the Englishman to make clothing from the fabrics of the world:

> Now I wyl were I cannot tel what.
> All new fashyons be plesaunt to me;
> I wul haue them, whether I thryue or thee.
> . . .
> I do feare no man; all men feryth me;
> I ouercome my aduersaries by land and by see.

The gist was that as a white male subject of the British Empire, you could "try on" the different ethnicities of the world — a swarthy Moor with a lascivious smile and dark skin, or a Chinaman with long, sinister nails. You could try on something else because you were a blank canvas.

My Uncle B. on my mom's side of the family (by marriage, not by blood) doesn't believe in "mixed marriage." That's how it was explained to me when I was seven. *Mixed* sounded vaguely delicious to my kid-ears. My main association was with the consumable variety: *mixed nuts. Mixed assorted candies*. But here, it just manifested itself in deliberate not-seeing. My brother and I in Florida over summer vacation, seated at our grandparents' table. B., the uncle, never acknowledging our existence. He remained as alien to me as perhaps I was to him. As I got older, it became a kind of game — a demented child pressing a finger to a bruise. I'd ask him to pass the carrots and some other less bigoted relative would fall over themselves to grab the dish for me before he could not-ignore my request.

B. has never mispronounced my name because he has never said it.

I acquired the nickname "Nesh" between the ages of seven and eight. Maybe because my friend R. thought my name sounded like the Hindu god Ganesh. Maybe not. I can't remember the origins, but it stuck. Though no one in my family ever called me "Nesh." They have their own variations of my name: My father, with his Indian accent, says it something like O-nesh-uh. My brother a little more nasal-y, like, Uh-nash-uh. And my mom like she's reading it straight out of a textbook, like she's instructing me how to say it every time: Aw-nay-shuh. *How do you say your name?* people ask, and I want to tell them: I don't really know. But this seems even more ridiculous than my name.

When I moved from Connecticut to North Carolina where I knew no one, I could have started over. But then I was marched in front of Mrs. Kelly's fifth grade class, already the odd one because I was starting halfway through the year. S. served as the emissary for the class when she stood up and said, "Hi. Do you speak English?" So it seemed better to be Nesh.

At any point after that, I could have insisted that I go by "Onnesha," but somehow it felt like asking people to call me by my real name was pretentious. I thought people would be like, *Ohhhh. Look at me. My name's Aw-NAY-shuh*. But I also didn't want to lie, so I had this little narrative that stuck with me until I was nineteen. When people asked me my name, I'd say, *MynameisOnneshabuteveryonecallsmeNeshbecause OnneshaiskindofdifficultsoyoucancallmeNesh*. I'd say it about that fast. People would just sort of shrug and be like, *OK. Hi, Nesh*. This is how it went until a professor asked me my name and I did my usual monologue. She just looked vaguely disgusted, like I had insulted her intelligence, and responded with, "Onnesha isn't that hard."

• •

"Onnesha" can also mean "illusion" — hinting at some truth behind a veil. It's a placeholder, a word you use to name a thing that you can only refer to by what it is obscured by.

• •

When I think of it now, I started going by Onnesha about six months after my closest friend died, when we were both nineteen. The sound of her voice on my answering machine enunciating my full name, a hint of mischief in her voice. I can picture the way her lip curls just the slightest bit. *On-nay-shuh. This is your friend Jew-lee-uh. Call me back.* That thing where, when the right person says your name, you blush because it is suddenly the most secret, magical word in the universe. So maybe I just wanted to hear someone say my name the way she did. Or maybe after you lose someone you really care about, it's like, fuck it. I don't care if you think I'm pretentious: *Say my name.*

When I dated E., we had this joke where he would call me Oshuhshashuhnaynay Rawchachacha in imitation of someone trying to pronounce my name and failing. His last name is Derkacz and is pronounced Dare-koch. Which rhymes with bear-crotch. I used to sometimes point this out, and he had a terribly fantastic sense of humor that stopped precisely here. The first time I said it, he just shook his head no. As though I had made some monstrous hybrid Holocaust/rape joke. I thought maybe he just didn't get it. *I don't mean* bare crotch, *like a naked crotch*, I clarified. *I mean bear crotch. Like the crotch of a bear.* The distinction seemed important to me, as though one phrase was totally stupid and tasteless, and the other was hilarious. Because who ever thinks of a bear's crotch? He had his own demons, having grown up with the bastardized Ellis Island version of his name — Dicker — before he legally changed it. But it always drove me nuts that I couldn't joke about his name. Like, what right do *you* have to be weird about your name?

Oshuhshashuhnaynay Rawchachacha.

When I was twenty-two, I did a radio interview. I was talking about an article I had written on the use of torture in Guantanamo. Before I went on air, the producer asked me how to pronounce my name and I told him. The radio host introduced me: Forgive me because the name is downright tough, but please welcome to the show Onnesha Roy-chowdery. Is that correct? *Close enough*, I say. I remember sitting at my kitchen table in San Francisco, my hands so shaky and sweaty I could barely pick up the mug of coffee in front of me. But when I listen to the audio now, I don't sound nervous. *Close enough*, I say. The tone dismissive, though whether it's of his ability to get my name right, or of the name itself, I'm not entirely sure. At the end of the interview, when I was off the air, the three hosts debate whether they got the name right, and what kind of name it is. For three minutes, they discuss:

> — I saw the name and it's got to be Indian or South Asian right?
> — I know immigrants. There's no way that's not an Indian name. And I love that Ben even gave it a slight Indian accent.
> — JR, what did it sound like she said on the phone?
> — Come on, it was a little Indian, wasn't it? Although Onnesha sounds like an African American name.
> — You gotta do the first name like it's a strong black name, O-nay-shuh. And then you gotta do the last name like it's a good Indian name, Roy-choud-huri.

During her Supreme Court confirmation hearings in 2009, Judge Sotomayor came under fire for having publicly stated that being a woman and Latina may influence her perspective.

"I think the system is strengthened when judges don't assume they're impartial," she says. "But [rather] when judges test themselves to identify when their emotions or experiences are driving their results." Senator Jeff Sessions of Alabama agitatedly adjusts his glasses and responds, "Aren't you saying... that you expect your background and heritage to influence your decision-making...? [Y]ou accept that there may be sympathies, prejudices and opinions that legitimately can influence a judge's decision?" Sessions concludes: "I reject such a view, and Americans reject such a view."

That slippery slope between "I" and "Americans."

Oh, to travel that distance in a breath.

A few years ago I wrote a short story that follows a first-person narrator. "I" standing in for any particular name. Though over the course of the story, we learn that the narrator — a writer — is at least partially Indian. At one point, she receives an email from her agent. Here is that scene as I wrote it:

> "Nobody biting yet," the agent writes, suggesting that I start something new — something that "takes advantage of your heritage.... How about a novel with an Indian-in-America theme? Sort of Jhumpa Lahiri-ish?" The room spins. I barely make it to the bathroom in time before I throw up the bourbon and remnants of spanakopita I ate at the bar. Staring in the mirror after I rinse my mouth with water, I take the lipstick on the counter and dab a reddish spot in the middle of my forehead. Then I bobble my head back and forth like my grandmother used to do when she was happily recounting a story. The red splotch looks like a target, a comic-book bullet wound.

With some encouragement, I (the real "I," or at least, the "I" writing this essay) shared this story and some others with an actual agent. After she read them, she sent me an email: "It's clear that you are a very talented writer with a bright future. That said, it's tough to sell story collections and the few that make it over the wall tend to have some overarching emotional arc or theme that connects all the stories. For instance, Jhumpa Lahiri's short stories have something larger to say about first generation Indian-Americans — about marriage, family dynamics, adjusting to a new country, etc., and I'm not quite sure what you're trying to say here.... I'd like to see more of your background woven into the stories."

I'm trying to tell you that "I" can be an exhausting thing to write. Because it's always already a conversation, even before we say "hello."

What I'm trying to say is that I do not tell you who I am without addressing what I assume you see. What I assume you assume about me. You probably don't even want me to do that. OK. I'll stop.

I can't stop. And as a writer, what happens when you cannot take "I" for granted? When a certain level of awareness is not just present *on* the page, but *on the way* to the page. The weight of a name. What it could mean. The things it might obscure. And the sense that the act of choosing a single name, a singular narrative among the many possibilities, is a lie in itself.

Below my last name — which would never fit into the bubble sheets for standardized tests, was another section. I was eleven before I realized my error, having bubbled in the wrong label. Thinking "American Indian" describes me because I am a) American, while at the same time b) Indian.

I do not make the same mistake again in conversation:
"What are you?"
"Half-non-white."
"What's the other half?"
"Non-Indian."

• •

OK, I lied. Onnesha means "in search of knowledge." It is a good Bengali name, which is to say that, if you're not careful, you can be crushed beneath it. It is a name that suggests both the ailment and the cure, though it's sometimes difficult to tell the difference between the two.

• •

In Italo Calvino's story, "The Distance of the Moon," the narrator's name is mentioned only once. A palindromic quintuple of consonants on the page that mock any attempt at assumptions, let alone pronunciation, the reader might make.

> How well I know! — old Qfwfq cried, — the rest of you can't remember, but I can. We had her on top of us all the time, that enormous Moon.

Qfwfq tells of a time when the moon moves from a distant "O" in the sky to a glowing orb close enough to lean a ladder against. A far-off celestial sphere suddenly made tangible.

O. It's an unintentional nickname I've acquired in adulthood. A shorthand. "O," a friend will say — a round-mouthed pronouncement, bent by tone into astonishment or comprehension. The start of something. Then it's just a matter of figuring out what comes next.

Muriel Rukeyser

Eyes of Night-Time

On the roads at night I saw the glitter of eyes:
my dark around me let shine one ray; that black
allowed their eyes: spangles in the cat's, air in the moth's eye shine,
mosaic of the fly, ruby-eyed beetle, the eyes that never weep,
the horned toad sitting and its tear of blood,
fighters and prisoners in the forest, people
aware in this almost total dark, with the difference,
the one broad fact of light.

Eyes on the road at night, sides of a road like rhyme;
the floor of the illumined shadow sea
and shallows with their assembling flash and show
of sight, root, holdfast, eyes of the brittle stars.
And your eyes in the shadowy red room,
scent of the forest entering, various time
calling and the light of wood along the ceiling
and over us birds calling and their circuit eyes.
And in our bodies the eyes of the dead and living
giving us gifts at hand, the glitter of all their eyes.

Rion Amilcar Scott

Three Insurrections

I went deep into the Wildlands one day and when they found me, I was near death. My flesh generated enough heat to keep a power plant going for a month, probably. I burned at 107 as if my heart had been replaced by a tiny sun. The doctor tells me brain death begins at 106. He says this ashen-faced, surprised I'm sitting up, conscious, bleary and dazed, but alive.

My parents sit across from my bed in Cross River Hospital Center, the place I was born. Here, too, I watched my son, Djassi, push himself into the world. I'm hoping the universe is not angling for some sort of weird irony, making my place of birth also my place of death.

Monique and Neville Samson, two human beings yet one person. My father reminds me of when I was four and I hit my older brother, Blair. Daddy asked me why I did it and I said, Dad, you know I'm brain-damaged.

Now you are, he says, cackling, leaning into my mother as she taps his arm and tells him to hush.

This is serious, Mr. Samson, the doctor says.

He tells me it's probably malaria or CHIKV, or dengue fever or something else you can't get in America. Don't believe any of that, please. I just went into the forest; I didn't leave the country. Though it's true that mosquitoes have never been my friend, what's really going on is that Cross River is trying to kill me. The doctor talks and I can feel my heart beating at a rapid speed and the heat from my skin is burning my sheets, but that's just the delirium. I think of the times I visited my godmother and cousins with my grandmother—my mother's mother—in Trinidad when I was young. The trucks driving by at night spraying white smoke into the air. Smoke seeping through the tightly drawn jalousies. The fleeing mosquitoes seeking refuge in the house my mother grew up in, the same house her mother grew up in. The bugs hide for a while, but then all die away. For a week, no mosquitoes drink from me and all my old welts stop itching and fade from my skin. In due time the bugs return, swarming me late into the night. Maybe, I think sitting in that hospital bed, they put something deep inside me that's only coming to life now.

Mr. Samson! The doctor says.

Kin! my father calls.

I look up.

The doctor says: What were you doing so deep in the Wildlands anyway?

I tell the doctor I was looking for myself.

(I don't tell my father when he asks.

Nor my mother.

Nor my wife, Peace.

I whisper it to my son later because he's a baby and thus unable to speak it.

I'm not here to tell you about my time in the Wildlands either, so if you've come for that then I'm sorry, but you'll be disappointed. Remind me later, though, and I might tell you.)

My father breaks the silence: Only two types of people does go that deep in the Wildlands, you know: fools and madmen.

You forget the wolfers, my mother replies.

What you think they are?

What about Blair? I ask. He think he a wolf hunter.

My father schupses.

A set of chupdiness, he mumbles. He a fool too. We only have one sensible child, Monique. Laina would never have go so deep in the Wildlands. Your brother and sister call yet, Kin?

Of course not.

My father sighs.

My father talks, but he never talks, you know. When we get silent and it's just hospital sounds around us, I ask him to tell me about his father. He pauses and says, What's there to say, boy? Then he becomes quiet and offers to watch Djassi so Peace can visit. Peace is the last person I want to see.

Like, Pop, I say, you tell me the funny stuff, like when that white guy beat up the ref at the soccer game —

Never see a cutass like that.

But what about the other stuff, huh Dad?

My mother says she'll go to my apartment to watch Djassi. Before either my father or I can object, she's out the door. It's just me and Neville Samson.

What's there to say? he says again. What you want to know, huh?

Like tell me, Dad — (I feel the fever bubbling through me like steam, burning my brain; I imagine it rising from the top of my skull on a bed of hot, white smoke) — tell me how we got to Cross River.

The pipe and the book. Is the book first and when I forget the book is the pipe that tell me go Cross River.

..

Is like history put its hands on my back and shove me from the sidewalk into the street, Kin. I was always an athlete so my mind does go back to that often. Stay on your feet. That's what I keep thinking. Like I'm on the football pitch and some guy's running toward me. I had a coach used to say, The most persistent rewards go to those who stay on their feet. But this, this is nothing like I ever seen, you know. These people out there rocking and flipping a car. We were like bees, Kin. All of us. Thousands upon thousands of bees waking up to find our queen get she head chop off.

You see you, all delirious and half-crazy? That's how everybody was on that day. I'll never forget April 5, 1968. The fourth was like a dream. Fuzzy, confusing. But the fifth was real. Martin Luther King dead.

I couldn't tell you why I was out there, in truth, Kin. Some people wanted to take a piece of whitey and call that justice. An even trade, you know. Some wanted the things they couldn't get on a regular day: television sets, jackets, scarves, food, all that. And then some of them was craving the fire, the burn. I don't know, boy. Maybe I wanted some of all of that. Too much to name, I guess. All I know is that I'm angry like everyone else. Whatever was in them was in me. I felt that buzzing like bee wings inside me. Wasn't no, I a Trini and you a Yankee. I a Trini and you a negro. Naw. Before I open my mouth they treat us all like niggers. That's it. Ain't take long to figure that out.

Wait, I go get to the pipe in a minute.

So, Kin, you wouldn't believe the amount of smoke they have rising up above DC. Smoke for so. They burn everything and most of them buildings stay like that for thirty years. I tell you I ain't never see nothing like it. People running around, in and out of the broken windows of stores. Ain't no police anywhere. I was over there near Florida and Rhode Island, just watching, boy. I live on R Street, so it not too much of a walk. People screaming and waving they arms. I just watch. Take it all in. Telling myself to stay on my feet.

The fires, though, remind me of the book. The cover self like it on fire. Sure did set fire in my mind when I was in teachers' college back home. *Three Insurrections*. It flit through my head at that moment. I ain't see that cover in about fifty years now, but it like I can see it right there in front of me. I ain't see that book for maybe two, three years, but it's in my mind's eye clear, clear. I know what I see, Kin; those exact flames from the riot is the same flames that was on the cover of that book. What they describe on all those pages is what I see in that city. I wish I could go back to that moment in the library at the teachers' college when I'm holding that book, drinking those pages, yes.

Before I could take it in, fully appreciate the moment, I feel a bump at my shoulder and is stumble I stumble.

Something in my heart start to flutter like I go die right there in this strange city in this strange country. I say to myself, *Boy, what kind of mistake you make coming here?* Like it's a football match and I make the play that lose the game, that's how I feel, but this is serious. All this is a second. Then I feel a hand grab my arm. Pull me up.

It's Charles. Now, Charles live on my block. He don't say much. Quiet eyes always searching. He sit outside on his stoop most of the time and he sit still, nearly a gargoyle. When I see him, we exchange two or three words, but them words got whole worlds inside them. Me and he born oceans apart, but we understand each other.

His hand the only thing stopping me from hitting my head on the concrete.

Neville, what you doing out in all this?

I pull myself to my feet.

The man only talk peace and they shoot him. But what is that?

So you see how they do us? They kill a man of peace. What you think they gon' do to regular negroes, huh? Neville, go home, brother. This all gon' blow over. They gonna build the buildings back and then they gon' be stomping us again. Go to class and get your degree and let us handle the shit, man.

Kin, Charles was wrong, you know. They ain't build nothing back. Not for thirty years. Remember when I take you to DC, begging you like hell to go to Howard. Nearly thirty years to the day, that's when they start taking down some of them buildings and putting something new there. What you think that do to people's minds, huh? How you think they feel living in the capital of the nation and it look like a war just happen?

But I respect the hell out of Charles. That winter before all this, I'm walking home and I see this man's hand. Not Charles, someone else. Something black in it. Black, black, black. Heavy. The thing look impatient. I ain't never see a gun in real life. My father ain't like those things. Never wanted them around.

You got any money on you, sir? he say, polite as ever.

I tremble. I scared. I nod. Reach for my wallet. Slowly. I not trying to anger that gun.

Thank you, he tell me, still with all the politeness his mother teach him. He never meet my eyes. To this day I think his gratitude was genuine, oui.

I see Charles the next day and I tell him what happen.

When all this go down? he ask, sitting there cool, cool, cool on his stoop. Yesterday? During the afternoon?

Yes. Bright as day, he jump out on me.

Charles nod. He grunt.

I go to pick up my mail the next day and beside to the letters and thing there's my wallet. Completely intact, except for the money, of course.

Standing there on that street in DC with the riot all around me, I watch Charles disappear into the world. I want to follow. I see the last flicker of him in between the people and I feel swept up. Dust in the gigantic broom of history. This how they want it, huh? Their negroes down bottom, frogs running from the river while children is chasing to crush them under they foot. Your grandmother used to say all the time — she ever say this to you? *What is joke for schoolboy is death for crapaud.* That was us, frogs scattering from the foot of a great white man.

I walk where I see Charles going; I don't see he, but I walk. Just walk. I don't know where I'm going. It's just walk, I walking.

So different than how yesterday start. Yesterday I walk with purpose, nearly stomping to class. Nothing on my mind but the test I'm bout to take. When I get to campus I see people huddled up. Seem like more people out on the Yard than usual. I don't think nothing of it. No time to think of anything but this chemistry test, anyway. Besides, wasn't nothing unusual about seeing people huddled up in intense conversation on campus. Howard was real. Someone always deep in political discussion. You look out and it's a sea of afros bobbing up and down furiously. Couple times we take over the campus. That's another story, though. What I'm getting at is Howard was the center of black life, at least for us, at least in DC. Wasn't strange to see Stokely Carmichael walking around the Yard. He graduate from there. You know he come from your mother's neighborhood in Port of Spain over East Dry River? You know that, right? She brag that they went to kindergarten together. What you laughing at, boy?

But I get by the library and I see Larry, your godfather. He say, Class cancel.

Class cancel? I stay up all night studying for this test. McGregor playing the —

All class cancel. You ain't hear? Someone shoot Martin Luther King.

Shoot? King? Who —

Larry shrug.

That's when that feeling start. That dislocation. It grow out of a feeling that I always had with me when I ask myself just what the hell I'm doing here. I still ask myself that when the winter whip in and I think bout how your Uncle Alton probably back home on the beach. That day I start wondering seriously why I'm here though, like why I come to a place where they kill a man of peace just for spite? Not even a year before, the football team at Howard, we play some team down South and afterward we try getting something to eat. Now alla we is Africans or from the West Indies, black, black, black. Wouldn't no one seat us, restaurant after restaurant. The coach, after he come from the last place, he get back on the bus, put he head down, and cry right there.

I ain't want to cry, but I ask myself why be here? Why I come to place that hate me? I forget the book. That's the answer to all that. The book. It flicker in my mind sometimes back then. Little shards of it. When I'm following the crowd in the chaos on that day after they kill King, I think of the book, a little bit. Not much though, but I think of it.

When I walk home from campus after hearing that King get shot, I start feeling dazed. My mind is alive. On fire. You should see all that was passing through there. I spend the fourth sitting in my room. I do schoolwork. I call your mother. I sleep. Dream. Wake and let myself get tortured by thoughts. Questions. *Why am I here?* Memories.

Right before I step on the plane to come over to America I hear about some negro bodies they find in the South all hung and twist up. Nowhere near DC, but still. Alton read the article in the newspaper to me in disbelief.

Neville, is sure you sure you want to take this trip?

Naw, Alton, I sure ain't.

But that wasn't the truth, Kin. Your Uncle Raoul had long split for Canada. Same with your Aunt Janice. And your Aunt Maisie was in England. I think Alvin was in Rochester by this time. When I get chance to go Howard I learn DC not too far from Cross River in Maryland — I read about Cross River in the book — so I go without thinking about it really. I want to see Cross River, the place of the Insurrection.

And since my father pass, I had been going and going and going. I had to slow it down just to get hold of my own thoughts.

The parties and the girls and the football and the cricket and there was a drama workshop I was taking and of course the teaching and teachers' college. I ain't expect to become no teacher growing up, you know. My father was respected in the teaching community. He was headmaster of the community school in our village, Tacarigua and he run the teachers' union for a while. So one of his friends, a fellow teacher, show up after I finish high school and say, Come, Neville, let we take a ride.

Before I know it I'm at the district office filling out forms, and Monday I get a letter assigning me to an elementary school in Tunapuna as an apprentice teacher. Teaching's in our blood, Kin. I was happy when you start teaching at Freedman's University. Your Aunt Janice taught and Raoul taught and even Blair for a time. That's your grandfather speaking through us.

I keep digressing. Where was I? Ah, yes. Out on the street. Me and the crowd. We marching now. Moving like an entity. Every few steps someone join up. Every few steps someone break off. I see people mashing up windows in stores. Some places got *Soul Brother* or *Black Owned* spray paint across the front. The crowd leave those alone. Most people just want to make a little mischief. Then they got some that's taking off with goods. To tell you the truth, I thought about breaking off, running through one of them stores. I just lose my job taking customer calls at the *Washington Post*. It was either play football or take a Sunday shift they ain't schedule me for. Guess which one I pick.

I get help from friends and thing, but it still hard. This before I start driving that illegal taxi while I was in law school. What you making your eyes big so for, huh? This after your brother born. You do what you do to survive. If you ain't see that with Djassi yet, you will.

I march steady, steady though. What go through my head is what my father would say he see me ransacking a store. I imagine Vernon Samson watching me.

My father. Boy, what can I say? I loved him. A lot. We were close. All of us were. Everyone have his own relationship with Daddy. He was a man without a past. You think I quiet about my old days. I an amateur next to he. After he pass, Maisie tell me a little what she know. His father may have been Indian, half-Indian, something, but I never know any of his family. He was an outside child and when he come an apprentice teacher, they assign him, coincidentally, out San Fernando near where his father live. Daddy tell his father, I never ask nothing from you and you never give me nothing much, but I getting my career start, I need a place to live out here while I apprentice. His father have a reputation. Lot of people look up to him. The whole world can't know he have an outside child running round, so he tell him, Boy, I can't help you and please don't come back asking for nothing.

So Daddy cut off all ties and ain't speak not once of his father to us. A professor up at the teachers' college one time pull me to the side and he say, You look just like your uncle, boy. I just blink, not sure what he talking about. Later I find out it have a justice in Port of Spain, Garvin Samson, but I never knew the man.

Everything about Daddy was steady and quiet. He have his own way of teaching you, eh. I tell you when your father is the headmaster you have to be a little tough. Back in elementary school I was supposed to stay in class during the first ten minutes of recess to get some extra help in maths. My friend Kelvin schups and say, Why we have to stay inside while everyone out playing? Well, boy, three of us out of seven choose to go to recess when we supposed to be inside. Me, Kelvin, and John. We playing football and laughing it up during recess. We even go by the window and point at the fellas who stay. No one telling us nothing the whole time we playing. At the end of the day my father announce that he giving the whole school some free time. An hour to play outside instead of sitting in class. Everyone start clapping and laughing and thing.

We get up and my father say, John, Kelvin, and Neville, please step to the front. Instead of the ten minutes we was supposed to have on lessons we spend the whole hour going over maths, listening to everyone outside, watching people come by the window and point. Daddy, boy.

Now later, when I get older and I'm in line for a scholarship to go London, I make the score, but they give it to some white boy in my class. Teacher say, Neville got the brains, but he too fast by he mouth. He not England material. Well, Kin, I feel defeated. Deflated. You hear certain things, like one of the Irish priests who teach in my high school always telling us that negroes in America too out of place and thing, but that's the first time I was make to feel . . . look, I was known to not hold my tongue. I wasn't no shrinking violet. Teachers and them don't like that. After that happen I just stop doing the work. I do it, but I do it in ten minutes before I go play football or cricket and it show when my marks come.

Daddy call me to his office in the back of our house and say, You comfortable with that?

I say, No.

I mean, Kin, what you think I go say?

Then he pause and he look away and he sigh. He say, You shouldn't be comfortable with those marks. But you going to be a big man soon. I can't tell you what you should be comfortable with. You have to decide what sort of man you going to be. Someone who comfortable with these sort of marks or someone who want to show the world what kind of light he got inside.

He ain't say no more, but I tell you I never brought home no marks like that again. He ain't have to rant and yell like . . . well, like I used to when you was being hard-headed. I guess I coulda take a lesson or two from him, but you was something else, Kin.

It's not long after that — well, it's not along after that that Daddy —

When he pass we was all together. Except Raoul. He was off in Canada already. It was strange for us to all be in the house at the same time. Except Alton, we was all grown or nearly grown. So much running around to do. It was the Christmas holiday or thereabouts and Daddy come home saying he not feeling too well. I remember there was a community meeting to attend to that night; he and your grandmother was very active. Mom go without him and let him rest and it happen after she get home. I hear she call out, Come, something happening with your father!

We rush in, all of us, and —

And well, boy, that is why you never get a chance to meet your grandfather. I happy as hell I get to wrestle with Djassi and all the rest of the grandchildren. I know your grandfather would have loved y'all like nothing else.

All that going and going and going. Never holding still from after Daddy's funeral to the time I left the island. All that stop me from dealing with how sudden, how unfair it was. Becoming a father ain't even offer me space to deal with it. I ain't even realize that I never reconcile it until you make me talk about Daddy right now. Even after I leave the island, there was school and football and shutting down the campus and getting adjusted to America and then they kill the King.

For that somebody must pay. So the riot happening all around me. It feel like j'ouvert morning. A swarm of us walking down the street and don't no one know where we supposed to end up. I feel protected from the chaos, but a part of it too. Any moment the police go come break us up, I feel. Or someone in the crowd go start something. I don't know these people, but quick, quick, quick it come like all for one.

Our swarm, it move like a flock of birds. All these beautiful black people in motion. Moving and shifting with a kind of intelligence. When we reach the destination we just know it. That shining palace on the hill overlooking Rhode Island Avenue. Ha! The Safeway.

We get to the place and alla we stand there watching it. And the manager, a short, little, bald, pink, fat, white man in an apron standing out front. I recognize him and his tiny, condescending eyes. A black person ask him questions and he real curt. That man wouldn't let me return some bad chicken I bought there earlier in the day one time. You think they could act like that out Bethesda? Safeway had a lot to answer for, Kin. I hated going to that place.

Please don't do this, the manager say.

I'm thinking, Why put your life on the line for a bunch of groceries. He must think Mr. Safeway go cry big tears at he funeral. Some guys surround him and they start shoving him back and forth and all around, passing him from man to man like a basketball.

The manager pull away and run into the riot. Bad move. One of the fellas catch he and hit him one — whap! — to the back of his head.

I didn't feel bad about what happen to the Safeway. You go in there you never see one of us working in the front. The meat bad sometime and you point that out, you get one cussing from the manager or someone under him. Prices always a dollar two, three, five higher than some other places like the Giant, but it's not easy for me to get to the Giant most times. I never realize it before, but I resent Safeway like hell from the moment I start shopping there until the moment we standing in front of it. No one is talking, but as a group we decide the store's fate.

A teenager grab a big rockstone and crash the thing through the store window. I want to say, Hey! We not done deciding, but I guess we finish.

Something in me, maybe is something by my heart, it tell me to turn around. To go on home. But then I see it clear as clear, the man King standing there on the cover of his book with his arms folded. Title say, *Why We Can't Wait*.

I had it out on my desk in class one day while I was in teachers' college. I pick it out at the library. You know, you hear bits and pieces about what the negroes in America is doing. Striking and sitting down and thing, but I needed to know more.

The teacher come by and she tap my book. This why you didn't do so well on the last test, Neville?

But I get an eighty.

Oh, excuse me. I took it from your earlier work that you're not the type of student who is fine with an eighty. My mistake. Careful with this stuff you reading, Neville. Careful.

I take it back to the library that day and I ain't read it till I get to America and realize everybody reading these books. Teachers assigning it in class. People talking about *The Communist Manifesto* and thing. Howard was real. That afternoon when I take it back to the library I was supposed to go play cricket, but when I get to the library, I see the book. The Book. The fires burning on the cover. Like an animated thing, you know. Like the whole table on fire and when I sit down the flames start to speak the pages. *Three Insurrections*. I have a cricket match, you know, but who could remember cricket staring at all that beauty? I miss the damn game to read the book. All the insurrections were sewn together like a beautiful garment on each page. The Haitians have a insurrection. The Riverbabies — the Cross Riverians — they have an insurrection and there is one to come, and it's mentioned with the ones that happen like it a piece of threaded gold passing through the garment. I don't see my name, but I see me. I see you and you don't even exist. You just a vague daydream in the back of the mind of two people who was on the same island, but ain't meet till they travel thousands of miles to go to Howard. You was just a sperm that's fifteen-plus years from being manufactured and an egg resting inside your mother.

Something make me left that book in the library, though. Maybe is too much to take the way it make my mind spin and spin. I wish to hell I had grab it and run. From then on Cross River is burn in my brain. I never thought too much about what's to happen with me next. I knew I ain't want to stay teaching forever. Some people expected me to become headmaster like Daddy, take over where he left off, but that's not who I am, I knew that. Whenever I think about the future after that day in the library, I hear Cross River whispering behind my thoughts. Maybe it's always been there. I don't know. I wouldn't doubt it.

But what kind of people is this? I think. These Cross River folks bloody their masters and live free like they not afraid. The book talk about the Haitians, too, but I hear about them plenty. The Cross River negroes is new to me. I see my island in a footnote. Some Cross Riverians set off through the Americas, trying to export insurrection. Some even settle in Trinidad, the beauty just hold them, even though they have slaves all over to free. I don't know much about our history before Daddy. Maybe we come from Cross River? How I know our people ain't take part in the Great Insurrection? And that is what draw me and your mother back. Maybe. Who knows is all I'm saying, Kin.

Something about this book, Kin, you don't read it. You read it, but it make you live it, like a dream. I come a Haitian that day, then I come a Cross Riverian. And just like a dream I live that third insurrection, too, but when I close the book, when I leave the library, I forget what it's like in the third insurrection and then I must spend the rest of my life chasing it down.

After I read it, I say to Alton, This happen somewhere in America.

I sit there and retell the Cross River part of the book as if I make it up right there. I wasn't sure I didn't.

They burn down the plantation and the kill the masters dead, I say. Boy, they ain't teach us none of that up at St. Mary's, oui. And I suspect they not going to teach it to you neither.

Alton nod from politeness more so than interest. When was all this? he ask me, but I can tell he not that concerned with my answer.

Back in the 1800s, I say. Early part. I go' go back to the library tomorrow and get that book for you. They call it the Great Insurrection. Got a town standing to this day in America. They ain't never shut it down. I have to go get you that book.

Alton make he lips so and turn from me like he can't be seen with a liar.

The librarian shrug when I go back. It's not on the shelf. No record of it ever being in the library.

You sure? I ask.

Perhaps it was a patron's, she tell me, but I don't think it was. I look for it in bookshops off Eastern Main Road. Every time I see a bookshop I look for it. When I get to Howard, I dig through the library stacks in search of it. I still look for it to this day. Now you got the Internet and I look for it there, too, but no dice, Kin.

The smoke from behind that Safeway, I think it like what I experience when I read the book. You look at me crazy, Kin. When you ever know me to not be rational? I studied chemistry when I was at Howard. I'm a man of science, but you can't tell a feeling nothing 'bout science.

Them people in the crowd start to pelt one set of bricks and rocks and thing at the Safeway and then when they finish they swarm like a crowd of ants. I ain't hear no sirens in the distance. It occur to me I ain't see not one cop. Later they send the National Guard to lock down the streets, but DC belong to us right then.

I think about turning around, leaving the place to the people and they anger. Come back to the Safeway only when I need bread and milk. But the book. The book is the thing.

Someone pull me, Come on, she say, Come on. Don't stand there. Come on.

I don't think of my father. I don't hesitate. I do as she say, as the crowd say. I come right on. You should have seen these people throwing things off the shelves. People with arms full of cheese, socks, heads of lettuce. Anything they can take with two hands.

A man run past me; he bump me with his shoulder. One set of bread go flying all over the place. I apologize and we both on the floor collecting the bread. His ill-gotten bread. He tell me, he say, It's nothing, brother. It's nothing. Don't worry about it. Hurry up and get you something before the pigs come. Don't worry about me. Go on, man. Go on.

So I go on.

I see they got turkeys, but people and them tell me that's what you eat here in November. I ain't know if it's strange to be eating turkey in April. Then I get to the dairy part. But I don't need no milk, no cheese, no yogurt. I turn and see the bread. Got enough bread at home. I had just been in this place a few days before white people decide to blow the world up. Not much I need, yes. I had to stop and laugh. I never shop so carefully. Neville, I say, What the devil you doing in here anyway?

I had imagined riots differently. All the upheavals I read about, heard about, and now I was in the middle of one, like the rebellious slaves in the book. Like me when I experience the book. That's what the devil I was up to.

I wander around. Floating. Dislocated. I remembered that I had lived through the Haitian Revolution and the Great Insurrection, both. The book make it so. Don't look at me crazy, Kin. I know how it sounds.

I stumble to the tobacco aisle. Still I'm empty-hand, but here is the pipe lying on the floor. Finally the pipe. Someone knock it from the shelf. The wood on the thing look smooth and shiny. Plastic tip on the end. I take it out the bag and rest it at the corner of my mouth.

Lottie, I mumble to myself. Lottie! Lottie! I take on the voice of my blind grandfather. Living all alone on all that land on Eastern Main Road, and when your grandmother come to visit him, me and one or a couple of your uncles or aunts in tow, he always know it she. The old man ain't know much of anything else, not anything about his grandchildren or anything it have going on in the world.

Your grandmother warn over and over before we go inside, Don't get too close. Your grandfather don't have all he wits.

Once on a good day, I could touch my grandfather, but that was early on in my life. By the time I was seven or so, only Mom could touch him or they say he was bound to fly into fits. That was something I ain't want to test. Mom always bring tobacco and dinner mints to calm him and when she walk in she call, Poopa! Though that magic sense he have already tell him it's she. Later when Grandpa get older and more agitated and excitable, he hold a cutlass tight in he hand when we walk through the door and he only relax his grip when he sure it's your grandmother and not bandits come to raid the house.

This day I watch the madman and his smoky, black eyes. This man who know nothing but his daughter and his short corncob pipe. That pipe. That pipe. It look nothing like the one I hold in my hand in Safeway, but it was everything like it if you ask me in the moment I'm standing in the aisle pretending I'm my grandfather. Granddad's house burn of urine and hot air hanging heavy. He call her name and his voice take on an edge until she respond or sometimes she just put a hand on his back.

Then he sit in his creaky chair and settle himself before reaching into the coal pot at his side to flip a piece of coal into his pipe. A couple puffs at that thing and he'd be content, peaceful. Granddaddy was always so precise, that burning ember flipping through the dark. It never burn him. Never sparked on the ground. Always flip into the mouth of that pipe.

This time it's me and Raoul and Mom. She wander about straightening up, then she go off to the kitchen to cook Granddaddy's food. I think is whisper I whisper when I turn to Raoul and say, Granddaddy's gonna burn this place one day.

Neville, you hush your mouth, your granny call from the next room.

Neville, you better hush your mouth, I mumble to myself in that Safeway tobacco aisle, and I'm back there smelling the smoke coming in from the street. Raoul disappeared and then my mother disappeared and then my grandfather was once again dead and gone, always like a spirit in a cloud of smoke. Sirens start screaming in a distance. There's a riot. A dead king somewhere shaking his head at all that burn in his name. There's the book and another insurrection somewhere, sometime. Police out there, maybe coming to save the Safeway and they don't mean no good for anybody.

I stuff the pipe in my pocket and run from the store back into the smoky streets and I ain't stop running till I at my door. All the while, my heart is beating fast, fast, fast in my ears like history shouting loud enough to deafen me, boy.

Not a day that go by after that I don't think about Cross River. That pipe, every time I look at it, it remind me that the book exist somewhere and another insurrection go be happening sometime. Thinking about Cross River make me late to my wedding. Laugh, Kin, but you almost wasn't made because of Cross River. We flirt with moving back to Trinidad, moving to upstate New York, but the only thing we take serious is moving to this town. I go to law school at Howard again and get a job and thing, but then when your sister is three or four and your brother is five or six, we pack up all our things, no job, no nothing. People ask me why I go Cross River, I say, We wanted to see the Insurrection.

I don't know what we think we go find; I don't know what we did find, but we find it.

I want you to remember this Kin: You are the only member of this family that is born into Cross River. The rest of we adopt it. Cross River is you. That moment in the aisle is you. Tell you the truth, when your brother, Blair, come a cop, I get disappointed. The son of Neville Samson a police? Naw. I feel like I ain't give him enough of what was in me in that moment during the riot. And your sister too damn reasonable for her own good. Sometimes, Kin, I think I give you too much of what was in me in that Safeway. You too damn miserable, but you, Akinsanya Abel Samson, you are the Cross Riverian Dream. I know you say that sound corny and thing, but when them people wrench themselves free, is you they think about.

..

We sit in silence listening to the hospital machines beeping and sighing. I wonder if the thoughts spinning wildly and crazily around my head are from the delirium or from my father's crazy tale.

He breaks the silence first by drifting off into a snore that startles and wakes him. I think of how much all this recollecting must have cost him.

Now you, he says.

Huh?

Tell me a story.

I don't have no stories like that.

Don't play the fool, Kin. You know what I mean. Tell me why you go quite out in the Wildlands.

Is nothing, boy, I say mimicking my father's accent, his voice, the shrug of his shoulder and the wave of his hand, the same way my face has always mimicked his own. Playing dead to catch corbeaux alive.

Solmaz Sharif

Desired Appreciation

Until now, now that I've reached my thirties:
All my Muse's poetry has been harmless:
American and diplomatic: a learned helplessness
Is what psychologists call it: my docile, desired state.
I've been largely well-behaved and gracious.
I've learned the doctors learned of learned helplessness
By shocking dogs. Eventually we things give up.
Am I grateful to be here? Someone eventually asks
If I love this country. In between the helplessness,
The agents, the nation must administer
A bit of hope: must meet basic dietary needs:
Ensure by tube, by nose, by throat, by other
Orifice. Must fistbump a janitor. Must muss up
Some kid's hair and let him loose
Around the Oval Office. *click click* could be cameras
Or the teeth of handcuffs closing to fix
The arms overhead. There must be a doctor on hand
To ensure the shoulders do not dislocate
And there must be Prince's "Raspberry Beret."
click click could be Morse code tapped out
Against a coffin wall to the neighboring coffin.
Outside my window, the snow lights cobalt
For a bit at dusk and I'm surprised
Every second of it. I had never seen the country
Like this. Somehow I can't say yes. *This is a beautiful country.*
I have not cast my eyes over it before, that is,
In this direction, is how John Brown put it
When he was put on the scaffold.
I feel like I must muzzle myself,
I told my psychologist.

"So you feel dangerous?" she said.
Yes.
"So you feel like a threat?"
Yes.
Why was I so surprised to hear it?

Wallace Stevens

Variations on a Summer Day

I

Say of the gulls that they are flying
In light blue air over dark blue sea.

II

A music more than a breath, but less
Than the wind, sub-music like sub-speech,
A repetition of unconscious things,
Letters of rock and water, words
Of the visible elements and of ours.

III

The rocks of the cliffs are the heads of dogs
That turn into fishes and leap
Into the sea.

IV

Star over Monhegan, Atlantic star,
Lantern without a bearer, you drift,
You, too, are drifting, in spite of your course;
Unless in the darkness, brightly-crowned
You are the will, if there is a will,
Or the portent of a will that was,
One of the portents of the will that was.

V

The leaves of the sea are shaken and shaken.
There was a tree that was a father.
We sat beneath it and sang our songs.

VI

It is cold to be forever young,
To come to tragic shores and flow,
In sapphire, round the sun-bleached stones,
Being, for old men, time of their time.

VII

One sparrow is worth a thousand gulls,
When it sings. The gull sits on chimney-tops.
He mocks the guineas, challenges
The crow, inciting various modes.
The sparrow requites one, without intent.

VIII

An exercise in viewing the world.
On the motive! But one looks at the sea
As one improvises, on the piano.

IX

This cloudy world, by aid of land and sea,
Night and day, wind and quiet, produces
More nights, more days, more clouds, more worlds.

X

To change nature, not merely to change ideas,
To escape from the body, so to feel
Those feelings that the body balks,
The feelings of the natures round us here:
As a boat feels when it cuts blue water.

XI

Now, the timothy at Pemaquid
That rolled in heat is silver tipped
And cold. The moon follows the sun like a French
Translation of a Russian poet.

XII

Everywhere the spruce trees bury soldiers:
Hugh March: a sergeant, a red coat, killed,
With his men, beyond the barbican.
Everywhere spruce trees bury spruce trees.

XIII

Cover the sea with the sand rose. Fill
The sky with the radiantiana
Of spray. Let all the salt be gone.

XIV

Words add to the senses. The words for the dazzle
Of mica, the dithering of grass,
The Arachne integument of dead trees,
Are the eye grown larger, more intense.

XV

The last island and its inhabitant,
The two alike, distinguish blues,
Until the difference between air
And sea exists by grace alone,
In objects, as white this, white that.

XVI

Round and round goes the bell of the water
And round and round goes the water itself
And that which is the pitch of its motion,
The bell of its dome, the patron of sound.

XVII

Pass through the door and through the walls,
Those bearing balsam, its field fragrance,
Pine-figures bringing sleep to sleep.

XVIII

Low tide, flat water, sultry sun.
One observes profoundest shadows rolling,
Damariscotta da da doo.

XIX

One boy swims under a tub, one sits
On top. Hurroo! The man-boat comes,
In a man-makenesse, neater than Naples.

XX

You could almost see the brass on her gleaming,
Not quite. The mist was to light what red
Is to fire. And her mainmast tapered to nothing,
Without teetering a millimeter's measure.
The beads on her rails seemed to grasp at transparence.
It was not yet the hour to be dauntlessly leaping.

Mark Strand

Anywhere Could Be Somewhere

I might have come from the high country, or maybe the low country, I don't recall which. I might have come from the city, but what city in what country is beyond me. I might have come from the outskirts of a city from which others have come or maybe a city from which only I have come. Who's to know? Who's to decide if it rained or the sun was out? Who's to remember? They say things are happening at the border, but which border is anyone's guess. They mention a hotel where it doesn't matter if you've forgotten your suitcase; there'll be another one waiting, big enough, and just for you.

Not To Miss The Great Thing

It was to happen. He knew it would happen. He would have secret knowledge of when that would be, and be there early to welcome it. The gates to the city were closed. A cloud lowered itself into the central square and disappeared into an unmarked alley. A large woman with sequins in her hair studied him from a distance. A cold rain fell on all the houses but his. Suddenly it stopped, and he walked out into the yellow light. Maybe it's come, he thought, maybe this is it, maybe this is all it is.

Virgil Suárez

Arroz

comes to El Volcan, the corner *bodega*
run by El Chino Chan,
along with the food rations
the people of Arroyo Naranjo, Cuba,
line up and wait for, in the meantime
they listen as Chan
calls out "*alo, alo,*" Spanish-Chinese
for *arroz*. Rice. I, six or seven, stand
in line, my mother next to me in the shade
of the *guayaba* trees, we watch as people
move in and out of the sun and heat.
Women fan their faces. Talk and gossip
buzz like the horseflies that fly up
from the ravine and brook. Chan tells
stories of when the great poet jumped
into the river and the villagers, to keep
the fish from gobbling up the poet, tossed in
rice dumplings wrapped in bamboo leaves.
Arroz. The blessing at weddings. Constant
staple with its richness of spirit. Sustenance.
Slowly the rations are filled and the line
moves and my mother and I reach the counter.
Behind it hang *papalotes*, kites made
of colorful rice paper, next to them
the countless oriental prints of carp,
egrets, tigers, and dragons. Chan talks
about the grain of rice kept in a glass
case at El Capitolio in the city, a love poem
etched on it in print so small one needs
more than a magnifying glass to read

what it says. Chan, rice, magic — the gift
of something different to pass the time.
Now, so many miles and years from this life,
in the new place called home, rice,
like potatoes, goes unnoticed when served.
Often, my daughters ignore it
and I won't permit it. Rice, I say, to them,
needs respect, needs worship,
their full attention, for blessed is that
which carries so many so far.

Arthur Sze

Sight Lines

I'm walking in sight of the Río Nambe—

salt cedar rises through silt in an irrigation ditch—

the snowpack in the Sangre de Cristos has already dwindled before spring—

at least no fires erupt in the conifers above Los Alamos—

the plutonium waste has been hauled to an underground site—

a man who built plutonium-triggers breeds horses now—

no one could anticipate this distance from Monticello—

Jefferson despised newspapers, but no one thing takes us out of ourselves—

during the Cultural Revolution, a boy saw his mother shot in front of a firing squad—

a woman detonates when a spam text triggers bombs strapped to her body—

when I come to an upright circular steel lid, I step out of the ditch—

I step out of the ditch but step deeper into myself—

I arrive at a space that no longer needs autumn or spring—

I find ginseng where there is no ginseng my talisman of desire—

though you are visiting Paris, you are here at my fingertips—

though I step back into the ditch, no whitening cloud dispels this world's mystery—

the ditch ran before the year of the Louisiana Purchase—

I'm walking on silt, glimpsing horses in the field —

fielding the shapes of our bodies in white sand —

though parallel lines touch in the infinite, the infinite is here —

Mary Szybist

Girls Overheard While Assembling a Puzzle

Are you sure this blue is the same as the
blue over there? This wall's like the
bottom of a pool, its
color I mean. I need a
darker two-piece this summer, the kind with
elastic at the waist so it actually
fits. I can't
find her hands. Where does this gold
go? It's like the angel's giving
her a little piece of honeycomb to eat.
I don't see why God doesn't
just come down and
kiss her himself. This is the red of that
lipstick we saw at the
mall. This piece of her
neck could fit into the light part
of the sky. I think this is a
piece of water. What kind of
queen? You mean
right here? And are we supposed to believe
she can suddenly
talk angel? Who thought this stuff
up? I wish I had a
velvet bikini. That flower's the color of the
veins in my grandmother's hands. I
wish we could

walk into that garden and pick an
X-ray to float on.
Yeah. I do too. I'd say a
zillion yeses to anyone for that.

Sam Taylor
From *The Book of Fools: An Essay in Memoir and Verse*

[Wikipedia, or the Late Style of Orpheus]

—Text quoted from Wikipedia article "Great Pacific garbage patch." Text bolded by poet Sam Taylor.

The Great Pacific Garbage Patch, also **described** as the Pacific Trash Vortex, **is a gyre** of marine litter in the central North Pacific Ocean located **roughly** between 135° to 155°W and 35° to 42°N. The patch extends over a very wide area, with estimates ranging from an area **the size of the** state of Texas to one larger than the continental United States; however, the exact size is **unknown**. This can be attributed to the fact that there is no specific standard for determining the boundary between the "normal" and "elevated" levels of pollutants and what constitutes being part of the patch. The size is determined by a higher-than-normal degree of concentration of pelagic debris in the water. Recent data collected from Pacific albatross populations suggest there may be two distinct zones of concentrated debris in the Pacific.

The Patch is characterized by exceptionally high concentrations of pelagic plastics, chemical sludge, and other debris that have been trapped by the currents of the North Pacific Gyre. Despite its size and density, the patch is not visible from satellite photography since it primarily consists of suspended particulates in the upper water column. Since **plastics break down** to ever smaller polymers, concentrations of submerged particles are not visible from space, nor do they appear **as a continuous** debris field. Instead, the patch is defined as an area in which the **mass** of plastic debris in the upper water column is significantly higher than average.

Some of these long-lasting plastics end up in the stomachs of marine birds and animals, and their young, including sea turtles and the Black-footed Albatross. Besides the particles' danger to wildlife, the floating debris can absorb organic pollutants from seawater, including PCBs, DDT, and PAHs. Aside from toxic effects, when ingested, some of these are mistaken by the endocrine system as estradiol, causing hormone disruption in the affected animal. These toxin-containing plastic pieces are also eaten by jellyfish, which are then eaten by larger fish. Many **of** these fish are then consumed by **human**s, resulting in the ingestion of toxic chemicals. Marine plastics also facilitate the spread of invasive species that attach to floating plastic in one region and drift long **distance**s to colonize other ecosystems.

Dylan Thomas

Poem

"If my head hurt a hair's foot
Pack back the downed bone. If the unpricked ball of my breath
Bump on a spout let the bubbles jump out.
Sooner drop with the worm of the ropes round my throat
Than bully ill love in the clouted scene.

"All game phrases fit your ring of a cockfight:
I'll comb the snared woods with a glove on a lamp,
Peck, sprint, dance on fountains and duck time
Before I rush in a crouch the ghost with a hammer, air,
Strike light, and bloody a loud room.

"If my bunched, monkey coming is cruel
Rage me back to the making house. My hand unravel
When you sew the deep door. The bed is a cross place.
Bend, if my journey ache, direction like an arc or make
A limp and riderless shape to leap nine thinning months."

"No. Not for Christ's dazzling bed
Or a nacreous sleep among soft particles and charms
My dear would I change my tears or your iron head.
Thrust, my daughter or son, to escape, there is none, none,
Nor when all ponderous heaven's host of waters breaks.

"Now to awake husked of gestures and my joy like a cave
To the anguish and carrion, to the infant forever unfree,
O my lost love bounced from a good home;
The grain that hurries this way from the rim of the grave
Has a voice and a house, and there and here you must couch and cry.

"Rest beyond choice in the dust-appointed grain,
At the breast stored with seas. No return
Through the waves of the fat streets nor the skeleton's thin ways.
The grave and my calm body are shut to your coming as stone,
And the endless beginning of prodigies suffers open."

Patrick Tobin

Cake

Annette the facilitator pretended to be Kate, a woman in our chronic pain support group who killed herself. We went around the circle, Annette in the middle, each of us given the opportunity to tell "Kate" what we were feeling.

Gail with fibromyalgia: "How could you give up?"

Stephanie with the botched spinal fusion: "You should have reached out for help!"

Liz with diabetes-related neuropathy: "What about your children?"

There were a lot of tears. A lot of hugging. Then it was my turn.

"I have a question," I said.

"For Kate?" Annette asked. "Or for me, Annette."

"Makes no difference," I said. "Is it true she jumped off the San Pedro Bridge?"

"Yes. But — "

"Is it also true that she landed on a Maersk cargo ship headed out to sea?"

Annette shifted uncomfortably. "Claire, we should focus on our feelings — "

"And is it also true that Maersk sent back what was left of her body in a Rubbermaid cooler, that the cooler was stuck in customs for a week before Kate's husband could take custody of it, that the cooler was stolen on the way to the funeral home because a homeless guy thought it contained a picnic?"

Annette looked around the circle at the horrified faces. When she looked back at me, she nodded.

I started applauding.

"Why are you clapping?" Annette asked, her big fat cow eyes filled with confusion.

"For a job well done. Personally, I hate it when suicides make it easy on the survivors."

• •

When I got home, there were two messages. On the first one, Annette said the group had stayed late after I left, that it had been a difficult session for everyone and she didn't want to minimize my feelings, but—

She and the others feel it's in everyone's best interest if I find another support group — perhaps one specifically to deal with my "anger issues."

The second message was from my ex-husband, Jason. He said he wanted to come by and pick up the last of his things. He asked me to call his assistant with a time when I won't be home, because he feels it's prudent that we don't see each other right now.

I'm sure his mother told him exactly what to say on the message because he never used to say things like "prudent." He always was a big mama's boy.

With all the excitement it was no wonder I was experiencing breakthrough pain. Breakthrough pain is my worst nightmare because it means the meds aren't working right.

Imagine the most excruciating thing you ever experienced. A migraine. A kidney stone. Giving birth.

All of these I've experienced, by the way.

Now try to imagine that the nerves involved in that pain are being pulled out by a sadistic fuck, one by one. No matter what you scream to make the sadistic fuck stop, he won't. The sadistic fuck just keeps laughing at you because he's enjoying your agony.

That, in a nutshell, is breakthrough pain.

• •

Guess who got a private room at Cedars with her very own morphine drip?

Morphine is like being wrapped up in warm towels fresh from the dryer. Morphine is like your mother rubbing your back when you have the flu. Morphine is like drinking cold water from a hose on the hottest day of the summer.

Who am I kidding? Morphine's even better than all that.

Thank you morphine.

Thank you.

Thank.

You.

Morphine.

Drug Induced Hallucination #1:

There was a boa constrictor slithering under my sheets. The snake tried to convince me that *As You Like It* is Shakespeare's most unjustly criticized play. I stared at the mound under my sheets and didn't move a muscle for hours. I knew if I made any movement the snake was going to stop arguing literary theory and devour me.

Drug Induced Hallucination #2:

A group of young kids was standing outside my room, talking loudly. They didn't go away. I got angrier and angrier.

I finally rang the nurse and told her to tell those fucking brats to move it somewhere else, if that wasn't too much fucking trouble. Or was I interrupting her goddamned fucking break?

That's when the kids started throwing a basketball against my door.

"Don't you hear that?" I asked the nurse.

She pulled the drip out of my arm and started jabbing the needle in her eyes. "I can't hear a thing."

Drug Induced Hallucination #3:

Kate walked into my hospital room carrying a cake with a bunch of candles on it. I told her I liked her new look.

"Thanks," she said. "I wish I could say the same about you."

"The morphine makes it kind of hard to fix myself up."

"You're probably wondering about the cake."

"I didn't want to be rude, but yes."

"Remember that time when Annette asked us what our dream would be if we didn't have chronic pain?"

"I always hated her drippy little exercises."

"You said your dream involved the Brazilian soccer team." Kate crinkled her nose in disapproval.

"And you said you wished you could bake your kids a birthday cake."

Kate lit the candles. "Everyone in the group cried after I said that. You didn't, though."

"I had my reasons."

"I know that now."

"To be honest, I wasn't that impressed with the whole Saint Kate thing."

"Saints don't jump off the San Pedro Bridge onto a Maersk cargo ship."

"Nice touch."

"I thought you'd like it."

Kate brought the cake over to me. "Make a wish," she said.

I closed my eyes and blew out the candles, even though I couldn't think of anything to wish for. When I opened my eyes, Kate threw the cake out the window and jumped out after it. There was a sickening thud and someone started screaming from the street below. A nurse ran into my room.

It took me awhile before I realized that the person screaming was actually me.

• •

The remote didn't work so my TV had been stuck on the Discovery channel the whole time. No wonder I was having nightmares about fucking boa constrictors. I told the mousy Filipina nurse to change the channel manually.

"No problem, your highness," she said.

"Ooh," I said, "somebody developed a spine while I was out of it."

She left the TV on the History channel after I told her to turn it to HBO. Touché, Imelda.

I watched a documentary about the demise of drive-in theaters in America. Apparently there aren't any left in California except for one in Barstow.

Jason took me to a drive-in theater when we were dating, back when we were both in law school at UCLA. He'd been mortified when I found the *Carpenters: Greatest Hits* in his glove compartment. I teased him about it, until he cued the tape up to "Close to You." He held me in his arms while we listened to the song — I'd never felt as safe as I did at that particular moment.

It was only the second time I'd ever gotten drunk. Captain Morgan's Spiced Rum and Coke, on top of a large carton of buttered popcorn. After I threw up, his car smelled like sour cinnamon toast. He gently stroked my hair and told me everything would be OK.

I was stupid enough to believe him.

• •

When I got home, I made two phone calls. First I called Rosalva, my cleaning lady, and asked if she had a driver's license. When I found out she did, I asked her if she wanted to make an extra couple hundred bucks.

Then I called Jason's office. I told his assistant to tell him I was going to be out of town tomorrow, so he could come by the house then.

I told her to tell Mama's Boy I'd changed all the locks, but I'd leave a key in the bottom of the deep end of the pool for him.

• •

For the road trip:
1. Vicodin.
2. OxyContin.
3. Methadone.
4. A nasal opiate from Glaxo that's still in the trial phase.
5. The phone number and Mapquest directions for a pharmacy in Barstow. Just in case.
6. A fifty-dollar ergonomic travel pillow I bought at Sharper Image.
7. A two-hundred-dollar lumbar support pillow I bought off the Internet.
8. Orange juice.
9. Chips.
10. My sunglasses.
11. A change of clothes. Just in case.
12. A bottle of Captain Morgan's Spiced Rum.
13. A six-pack of Coke.

• •

The drive to Barstow should normally take two hours, not five. I had to get out every twenty minutes to stretch. I felt like my breaks were starting to get on Rosalva's nerves.

"No, no, no, Mrs. Fine. Is OK," she said.

I told her I was still freaked out by the crow we killed near San Bernardino, the way it dived head-on into our car like a kamikaze pilot.

Rosalva acted like she was about to cross herself. "No more please."

"Sorry. We don't have to talk about the crow." I offered her some chips and a Coke and that seemed to improve her mood.

• •

The pain got bad near Apple Valley. That annoyed me. It also annoyed me the way Rosalva looked at me when I took my pills.

"Could you do me a favor?" I asked.

"Yes, ask me what you need."

"Don't call me Mrs. Fine," I said. "I'm divorced now so I don't want to be called Mrs. Fine."

"But what to call you?"

"How about Claire. That's my name."

"OK, Mrs. Claire," she said.

With a sweet smile. Oh, fuck it. She'll get it right one of these days.

• •

Rosalva loved *The Passion of the Christ*. I found it kind of weird to listen to all the torture through the small, tinny speaker. I started chipping off the polish on my toenails.

"You must be seeing this," Rosalva said, her eyes filled with tears.

"I *am* seeing this," I told her, as chunk number forty-five flew off Jesus' body. "I'm also seeing we're out of Coke."

She seemed relieved when I offered to go to the concession stand so she could keep watching the movie. It's OK, I get it: The Jews killed Jesus, so we should have to go to the concession stand during *The Passion of the Christ*.

• •

The desert night sky is dreamy this time of year — a deep purplish blue and stars that look like Christmas lights. The cold air hurt my lungs, but in a good way.

I crawled under the low wire fence behind the concession stand and walked through shrubs and gravel down to the train tracks.

What would Jesus do? I think if he were in my shoes he would lie down and wait for the next Union Pacific freight train.

• •

When you think you're going to die imminently, you choose your final thoughts carefully. I tried to think of beautiful things, like Michelangelo's *David*. A Bach cantata.

That got me thinking about the *Nutcracker Suite*. When I was a little girl, I danced as a mouse two years in a row. It's still one of my favorite pieces of music.

My thoughts turned to Jason.

I hated to admit it, but I did understand what he meant when he said I wasn't the only one suffering — right before he handed me the divorce papers he'd personally drawn up. It was hard at the time to react graciously to what he said, because, after all, he'd walked away from the accident with only a sprained shoulder.

But now — I can see.

I can see that we were both the wrong kind of people to deal with this kind of situation. Problems that could be solved by money: *that's* the most we could handle. Not the loss. Not the pain. Not all the thousands and thousands and thousands of pills.

Too bad Jason's such a mama's boy that he'd never take methadone, because it really does help take the edge off life.

I felt the low rumble of a train. Then I heard a voice, getting closer and closer.

"Mrs. Claire! *Ay Dios mío*! Mrs. Claire!"

I struggled to sit up and saw Rosalva scrambling towards the tracks. I tried to gauge how far the train was in relation to her distance from me.

"It's OK, it's OK," I said, "I just got tired and needed a rest."

• •

During the drive back Rosalva kept looking at me like I was going to jump out of the car.

"Knock it off with the attitude already," I said.

She scolded me in Spanish. I think she said something about how it was a good thing Jesus told her I went "loco."

I was thinking of the most profane thing I could say when the car started making a grinding noise. Right before the "service engine" light went on.

• •

The guy at the garage in Barstow said it was going to take at least three days to fix the car. He tried to explain the problem to me.

"I don't need to understand what a head gasket is," I said. "Just make the arrangements for a rental car."

Blank stare.

"OK," I said, "maybe you don't understand Triple A. I have the *platinum* coverage that gets me a free mid-size rental if repairs are going to take more than twenty-four hours."

"There's nothing open now," he said.

"Why? Is it a holiday?"

"It's nearly midnight. People have to sleep."

Now it was my turn for a blank stare.

. .

Inside a dark Greyhound bus, strung out on opiates, traveling through the high desert in the middle of the night, I started to feel like I was in a rocket flying through outer space. I stared at Rosalva while she slept next to me. She opened her eyes.

"Gracias," I said.

"Why?" she asked.

"For putting up with me," I said. "I wish I knew how to say that in Spanish."

"Sleep, Mrs. Claire." Rosalva closed her eyes again.

I heard muffled laughter from the back of the bus. I turned around and saw a group of teenagers passing around a joint. Everyone else on the bus was asleep. I waited a few minutes, the smell of pot becoming stronger.

I made my way to the back. The leader of the group, a girl with a bad tattoo of a python on her arm, glared at me.

"Toilet's broke, bitch."

Her friends laughed.

"I don't need to use the toilet."

She sneered. "Then beat it."

Her friends were enjoying the show. I leaned down into her face.

"I used to be married to a federal prosecutor in L.A. Even though I hate his guts, I have no problem getting on my cell phone and asking him to send a marshal to the bus station."

The sneer disappeared.

I pointed to the joint in her hand. "Is that just pot or did you morons cut it with something else?"

. .

I'd hoped the girl — Becky, a runaway from Idaho — wouldn't want to talk, but once we started on the second joint she wouldn't shut up.

"I want to be an actress," Becky said.

"Can I give you some unsolicited feedback?"

"Hell no."

"You're going to end up doing porn. Or worse. That's what happens to girls from Idaho like you."

"Gross! I won't do porn!"

"Right. Do any of these stars ever say in an interview, 'I ran away from Idaho when I was sixteen and ended up doing Hollywood movies'? No. That's what porn actresses say. Not Hilary Duff."

"I hate Hilary Duff," she said.

"If I had your body I would too."

"At least I don't look like you." She pointed at my face and arms with a vicious little smile.

"Give it time, honey. You'll get your own scars some day."

I asked if she had another joint.

"I hope you know these weren't free," she pouted.

I pulled out a hundred dollar bill. "Let's skip the soul baring. It's starting to get on my nerves."

• •

Becky finally passed out. The bus was absolutely quiet as we went down the Cajon Pass. The sun was just coming up. The San Gabriel Valley glowed from under an ozone shroud.

Rosalva woke up. She panicked when she didn't find me next to her. I waved from my seat next to Becky.

"Who is this?" she asked, eyeing Becky's tattoo.

"I'm starved. I want a yellow cake with lots of fudge frosting."

"I make one tomorrow."

"I want one the minute we get home."

"Mrs. Claire, I must go to my home. Later I come to your home."

I realized I had no idea where Rosalva lived.

"Downey," she answered. "You do not know this place I am sure."

"Isn't that where the Carpenters were from?"

"I have not met them."

When we sat down in our seats, Rosalva pulled out a brush and started combing my hair. I began to sing.

"Why do birds . . . suddenly appear . . ."

Rosalva smiled. "This is very pretty song."

"Every time . . . you are near? Just like me . . . they long to be . . . close to you."

• •

At the L.A. bus station I sent Rosalva to Downey in a cab. While I waited for my own cab, I noticed Becky's friends had deserted her. She walked up to me with a shy look on her face.

"What are your big plans?" I asked. "Oh that's right, you're going to be a star."

"Shut up."

"Want to make an easy hundred?"

She gave me a look of disgust. "I knew you were a dyke."

"I don't want to fuck you. I just want you to bake me a cake."

"You're a freak. You know that, right?"

"Can you follow directions on a package, or are you illiterate?"

"Am I what?"

"Jesus. Can you read? Do they still teach that in Idaho?"

A cab pulled up. I opened the door and waited for Becky. She studied my face, trying to decide if I was a good risk or not. I felt bad for her until my legs started killing me again.

I sighed. "Do I look like someone who could hurt you?"

"You're mean enough."

"You outweigh me by at least fifty pounds."

"Fuck you."

"Fine."

I got inside and gave the cabbie my address. We were driving off when I heard Becky's voice.

"Wait!" she yelled, running after the cab.

I didn't look at her when she got in the car. "Offer's fifty now."

"What?"

"You heard me."

"That's not fair."

"Life's not fair. Any more lip and it goes down to twenty-five."

• •

Becky decided to make the cake from scratch. We were at the grocery store right by my house, in the baking section. I'd become distracted by the Disney-themed birthday candles.

"Do you have baking powder?" Becky asked.

"I'm not sure." I was starting to lose focus. "Is that the stuff you put in the fridge to keep it from smelling?"

Becky rolled her eyes. "That's baking soda."

"Then I don't think I have baking powder."

"Who doesn't have baking powder?"

"People who order out, that's who."

"You're pathetic," Becky said, while were standing in the checkout line.

"You're only just now realizing that? God, you *are* stupid."

"What about booze?" Becky asked.

"Can you handle liquor? I don't want green puke all over my carpet after you drink a whole bottle of Midori."

"Why are you such a cunt?" she hissed.

"Paper or plastic?" the clerk nervously asked.

• •

While Becky made the cake, I went through the house. The last of Jason's clothes were gone. All the tools were missing — not that I'd ever use them. All his books were out of the den. With his collection gone it really exposed my intellectual laziness — Clive Cussler no longer propped up by *The Collected Works of Shakespeare*.

I found the picture on the desk, the framed photo of Jason and me and the twins. We'd hired an expensive photographer, a guy who does fashion spreads for *Los Angeles* magazine. The year before the accident, for our holiday greeting card.

I picked it up and studied our faces, until none of us was recognizable. I thought I'd made it clear to Jason he could keep the picture.

I called his office.

"Mr. Fine's not in. Would you like to leave a message?" his assistant asked.

"Tell him he won."

"Won what?" The assistant sounded nervous.

"He'll know," I said, before I hung up the phone.

• •

I took so much methadone I just barely made it to my bed. Becky yelled from the kitchen.

"Where's the fucking booze?"

"Be resourceful!" I yelled back. "You need to be resourceful!"

My last thought before I passed out was that maybe primitive cultures are right — I think the camera did steal my soul.

• •

When I woke up, Rosalva was wiping my face with a cold washcloth.

"What time is it?" I asked.

"Too many hours," she said.

"Is the girl still here?"

"No. I think she stealed."

Rosalva helped me get up. We discovered that Becky had taken my purse, all of my jewelry, all of the liquor, and the entire stash of pain medication, including the methadone.

How did she find the methadone? I'd completely underestimated her.

"I call the police," Rosalva said.

I stared at the frosted cake on the kitchen counter, covered in plastic wrap. "No."

"She does wrong when you are sick! This is bad girl!"

I dabbed my finger on the top of the cake and tasted it. Homemade fudge frosting. A little on the sweet side, but definitely homemade.

• •

It's impossible in L.A. to find out where someone lives if they haven't given you the information. The white pages are useless; 411 is a fucking joke. I needed to talk to a human being and not Verizon's annoying computer, so I called Annette.

"And how are we doing Claire?"

"We're doing *great*."

"Well, that's super. Did you find another support group?"

"Funny you should mention that. Ever hear of Gloria Allred?"

"Uh, well, yes, I have."

"Because I've decided to sue you for discrimination."

"Goodness. A lawsuit?"

"Just kidding. I'm calling to get Kate's address."

"I don't think I'm allowed to give out that information. Was there something else I could help you with?"

"That's hardly possible."

"Well, I'm certain I can't give you that information. I'm sorry."

"Remember when I said I was kidding about the lawsuit?"

"Uh huh."

"Now I'm not kidding."

• •

The address was in Palos Verdes, for a house that looked like the bastard child of a mansion and a small hotel. Rosalva, bless her heart, drove me there in the mid-size rental. I told her to wait for me in the car.

"I help you, Mrs. Claire."

"Thanks, but I need to do this by myself."

I wonder what Kate's husband will say. I have to remember his name before I ring the doorbell. Ken? Ben?

Fuck it. I'll just mumble something.

I hope he doesn't freak out and think I'm a crazy person for bringing a cake with cheap Disney-themed candles. Will I actually tell him it was something Kate had wanted to do for the kids? Jesus, I hope he doesn't start crying, or worse, ask me to come in to meet the family.

I stand outside the front door, my hand ready to press the bell. I hear children's voices inside. Lots of children.

I take a deep breath.

Phillip B. Williams

Luminous, Whatever Honey

I go to twist the knob of a burning skull
that burns because the canyon sun has touched
curve after curve of the hard, soiled thing
into luminosity, as though veins ran courses
around the buffered ivory of socket and tooth,
rounded where thinking broke loose.
Coyote skull? Fox skull? I'm too ignorant
to know. The elaborate bone is circled by opulence:
cactus blossoms, a beetle's green carapace. My thumb
falls into where sight's gone hollow. My fingers
fondle the spinal gap for whatever sap's
left over in the desiccated jaw. Whatever honey
was eaten has calcified, as though hunger has frozen
under skin, over thought, in the tremble of my hand.

James Wright

All the Beautiful Are Blameless

Out of a dark into the dark she leaped
Lightly this day.
Heavy with prey, the evening skiffs are gone,
And drowsy divers lift their helmets off,
Dry on the shore.

Two stupid harly-charlies got her drunk
And took her swimming naked on the lake.
The waters rippled lute-like round the boat,
And far beyond them dipping up and down,
Unmythological sylphs, their names unknown,
Beckoned to sandbars where the evenings fall.

Only another drunk would say she heard
A natural voice
Luring the flesh across the water.
I think of those unmythological
Sylphs of the trees.

Slight but orplidean shoulders weave in dusk
Before my eyes when I walk lonely forward
To kick beer-cans from tracked declivities.
If I, being lightly sane, may carve a mouth
Out of the air to kiss, the drowned girl surely
Listened to lute-song where the sylphs are gone.
The living and the dead glide hand in hand
Under cool waters where the days are gone.
Out of the dark into a dark I stand.
The ugly curse the world and pin my arms
Down by their grinning teeth, sneering a blame.

Closing my eyes, I look for hungry swans
To plunder the lake and bear the girl away,
Back to the larger waters where the sea
Sifts, judges, gathers the body, and subsides.

But here the starved, touristic crowd divides
And offers the dead
Hell for the living body's evil:
The girl flopped in the water like a pig
And drowned dead drunk.

So do the pure defend themselves. But she,
Risen to kiss the sky, her limbs still whole,
Rides on the dark tarpaulin toward the shore;
And the hired saviours turn their painted shell
Along the wharf, to list her human name.
But the dead have no names, they lie so still,
And all the beautiful are blameless now.

Charles Wyatt

Excerpts From *The Spirit Autobiography of S. M. Jones*

I was born in 1836 with a veil over my face, a fact to which some might attribute the story I am about to tell. I write not to gain eccentric notoriety, but do so out of a good and honest heart, through the influence of some mysterious power. The candid reader may accredit all that is herein written, for they are veritable facts.

Invisible Kittens

Evenings we often sat and read, our conversation desultory as the sounds of the log falling to pieces in the fireplace. I liked those quiet times, especially when Mother would tell us her stories. On the occasion I have in mind, I was seven or eight, not long recovered from my illness — Tommy was playing with his lead soldiers, arranging them in rows like the corn standing in the back of the garden. I suppose I was tormenting him by secretly causing them to fall when Mother put down her sewing.

Mother began to tell us one of Tommy's favorite stories about the little people — the little people lived in the garden and were small enough to hide in milkweed pods. Like mankind, they made mischief and did good in more or less equal measure, but were most amazing in their ability to avoid detection. They could simply tell when we were going to look their way. "Can't you feel when someone is watching you?" Mother asked us. "The little people can feel when you are about to see them, and they hide."

"Why can't I hide like the little people?" Tommy complained. "Sylvester always finds me when I hide."

"Then you must persuade them to teach you their art."

"But no one can see the little people. How could I catch one?"

"The little people would never help you if you try to catch them, but they listen from their hiding places. Sometimes they teach children how to hide the way they do. But you would need a better reason than Sylvester always finding you."

"I know a good reason," Tommy said, "but I'm not going to tell."

"You don't have to tell me," I said. "You have to tell them and you don't know where to find them."

Mother said we might hear them singing among the crickets (whom they tended) and katydids (which they did not tend, as anyone could tell by listening). And later, Tommy and I began to play a game of turning suddenly in the hope of catching one unaware. Sometimes I felt I had seen a small figure, especially in the tall weeds near the fence row, but Tommy's sightings, and this was usual in our games, were both more frequent and fervent than mine. This night, Mother's story was of the little people sailing over the meadows, using silken threads they had stolen from spiders. They were bringing secrets of the world to the hiding children, the children they had taught the secrets of their invisibility.

I had chosen a small rocking chair with flat comfortable arms, and I had grown quite drowsy as the story developed, as Mother's stories often did, into a listing of all the plants of the meadow and the properties of healing and harm they contained. Suddenly I felt something fall into my lap. Had I been touched by a moth, or had some projectile winged its way past me, perhaps in retribution for my recent mischief? I looked at Tommy, but he seemed to be innocent. Sensing my gaze, he looked up from his squadrons.

"What is it?" he asked.

"I don't know," I said. "Something fell into my lap, but it's not here now."

Then something brushed against my hand on the arm of the chair away from Tommy. It was fairly dark in the room because the fire had died down, but I could see that there was nothing there.

"Who threw that?" I asked. And to the ensuing silence, I demanded, "Who . . . who threw that?"

At this point, Mother, who had taken up her mending again at the end of her story, suggested that we go to bed. I was a nervous child. I would always be a nervous child, inclined to disrupt her quieter moments. After she had tucked us in, and we had said our prayers, and only the candle in the hallway was left burning, I felt again that soft impression of something falling on my bedclothes.

"Did you throw that, Tommy?" I asked. Already half asleep, he only mumbled.

"Wake up, wake up. There is something strange going on." As I spoke I groped about the bedspread, searching for the object that had fallen on it. Then I grasped it, something small, furry, and wiggling — unquestionably a kitten. I could feel its tiny claws, but it made no sound at all. I was filled with the kind of loathing that the sight of maggots brings, part from the suddenness of the vision, part from sympathy for the once living thing they have so awfully transformed. The eye refuses to take it in. The mind cannot deal in swarming things. I felt there was some like thing in my hand. I threw it out of the bed. When it should have struck the floor, it did not. At least, there was no sound at all. Tommy began to snore softly. I felt another small thump on the bed, and then another. Groping around me, I gathered them up. It was dark, but not so dark that I could not see what I was grasping: nothing. But I could feel the fur and the tiny squirming limbs, ending in needle-sharp claws. One by one, I threw them out of the bed. Again, there was no sound.

"Tommy, wake up," I hissed repeatedly, as they came like a slow rain or hail against the bedclothes.

"What is it?" He sounded awake by now. I continued to perform my charade of gathering, grasping, and throwing. "Get down on the floor and feel around," I whispered. "There should be something there. I am throwing them."

"Throwing what?"

"Kittens. You should be able to feel them."

"Are you awake?"

"Yes, yes, I am awake. What can you feel there? Reach under the bed."

He struggled out from under the covers and groped about on the floor. It was a cold night, and I could hear him shivering.

"Well, what do you feel?"

"Nothing. There isn't anything here. What in the world have you been doing?"

"Come here then. I have gathered them all around me."

Then when Tommy came over to my bedside, I realized that they were gone.

"They were kittens. And they were invisible. I could feel their tiny claws and teeth. And when I threw them, they disappeared. Well, they finished disappearing. I threw them and there was no sound at all. But they kept falling on my bed."

"You were dreaming," he said. "I have had dreams like that before. In fact," he said thoughtfully, "I have had a dream very like this. Invisible kittens. But I had forgotten it."

"No, it was no dream. Come here and bring the candle." And by its light, I showed him the scratches on my hands and wrists.

The Magic Box

When Tommy was five and I was six, we were playing in the attic one day and found the little box. It was a large attic and the cat had favored it to hide her kittens. All week we looked for them, getting ourselves dirty enough to be scrubbed raw by Peach, who still did not seem to mind our playing there. We found them finally, but their eyes were closed — they were too tiny for us to play with. The box we found near the cat's nest was sturdy but old, about eighteen inches square. I suppose the wood was oak or maple. It had a lid and hinges, but these were broken, so the lid merely lay across the top. The box seemed ordinary, but useful, and we included it in our games, using it to store marbles and the like. Then, when we were playing at soldiers and had taken them all out of the box, Tommy gave a queer look, and laying his hands on the lid, which he placed back on the box, said, "Who's there?" And with this utterance, the lid slipped off the box under his hands. I thought it was a good game and asked if I could try it, too. "Who's there?" I called dramatically, and the lid bucked under my hands as if the box contained something alive. I was as shocked as I had been the year before when the heavy door of the feed store in town had closed on my hand and I could not cry out because of the pain or the surprise. Finally I was able to speak. "Tommy, what was in the box?"

"There's nothing in the box," he said simply, holding it for me to see.

The inside of the box was bare and a little dusty. I felt carefully around it to detect some secret feature, but the boards were plain.

Satisfied that there was no snake or creature in the box, I was content to ignore its tendency to toss off its lid. We kept the lead soldiers, special stones, and arrowheads in it and occasionally brought it out for play.

One Sabbath there was a neighbor visiting at the house, named Fitzpatrick. He was, I think, an especially strong young man. I remember particularly his bulging arms. Tommy and I were playing on the floor, and when the box was emptied of our playthings, the "who's there" game commenced. We would hold our little hands on the lid, call out "who's there," and off the lid would tip. Farmer Fitzpatrick came over to us and asked us what we were playing. We explained the game and he asked if he could try, also. Laying his hand on the box lid, he called out, "Who's there?" Instantly the lid tipped off the box. With a look of astonishment on his face, he picked up the box and examined it minutely. Then he asked if he might repeat the experiment. This second time, he laid both his large rough hands on the box lid, and called out the words with rather more an inflection of genuine curiosity than before. Again, the box lid tipped off, this time causing Farmer Fitzpatrick to fall back with a heavy thump.

I remember that Mother had come into the room, causing Farmer Fitz to swallow some of the epithets he had been applying freely to the box and its unknown inhabitants. "May I try one more time?" he asked politely. We offered no objections. He took the box to the doorway, placed it on the jamb rock, and bracing himself above it, held down the lid with both his hands, his muscles straining in anticipation. "Who's there?" he called through clenched teeth. At these words, the lid came off the box again, violently pitching Farmer Fitz out the door and onto his backside in the dusty lane. He lay there for a moment as if the wind had been knocked out of him, but when my mother inquired if he were hurt, he slowly got to his feet, dusted himself off and said, "I am satisfied." With those words, he turned on his heel and did not visit our house again.

At dinner, Father smiled at our story, but then became thoughtful and said the box would have to go. Tommy and I protested tearfully, and Mother suggested that it was a useful box, that she could keep it in the kitchen. Father assented to this arrangement.

Now Mother and Peach often sang as they bustled about preparing meals. The little box was placed in a corner; and when the women sang, it would make a tapping noise, its lid jigging along in perfect time. Mother stopped her work, and, after wiping her hands on her apron, picked up the box and held it before her.

"Is anyone in there?" she asked. "Can you speak?"

From inside the box came a loud sound of hissing, just like the hissing of a goose. Mother put the box back in its corner and did not look inside, as the others had done. Soon she and Peach were singing again and the box resumed its rhythmic tapping.

One day I noticed that the box was no longer in its corner in the kitchen and I asked Mother what had become of it.

"I have put it away," she replied, bustling about and not looking at me. "Your father has decided it is unseemly for us to have a singing spirit box, or whatever it might be."

"But where have you put it?" I cried, for it was like an old pet to me.

Mother would not answer me, but from that day on, the door to the attic was locked, and Peach would not let us play there.

Hellmoffring

> What is your name what is my name whats in a name there under a rock you see them spelling it spelling what spelling isnt telling who was that hellmoffring yes my name is hogmoffring who was I indeed I was an indian chief a large dog large red dog with bristles in a quiver like to shake a snake who is with me oh we are several here where here its not cold its like the barn falling from the hayloft all the time whats it like all the time falling you get used to it yes hellmoff what does it mean it means this bush not that why should I tell you yes hogmiff well what is yours the bear the bear the bear came over oh we can talk we like to sing who who who my frings my wings my dings my my awfuls oh play for us sylvester slay for us pylvester

The writing began, as did all things really, in those days when Tommy and I were together. Tommy could do it and I learned that I could as well. It was simply a matter of sitting quietly, pen in hand. "Put yourself away," Tommy said, and then the pen would move. At the time, Tommy could only write his name, but he discovered the trick, nonetheless. He would hold the pen loosely and it would dart about the page. He insisted that it was doing those things of its own accord. So, at his behest, I held the pen and made a blank of my mind, something I was surprised to discover I could do easily. Then the pen would move and often wrote gibberish and vile, bad words. Still, it was amusing, and we played at it often enough until Mother caught us at it. She said it was wrong and sacrilege, and it seemed suddenly to us that it was so. We were not punished that I can recall, and that was the end of it.

That was the end of it until about the time of my discourses with Dudley upon the spirit world. I found myself drifting off over Latin exercises or even the notes I sometimes wrote at end of day on my practicing. Hellmoffring is the name I use, but it called itself by many names, asking and answering its own questions (although its answers were seldom satisfactory). It became a nuisance for me because I sometimes became thoughtful when I was writing in my journal, and then I was likely to come to myself over a page of such scribbling — and odd it was, all swirls and swoops as if the pen itself had taken on the character of a water beetle. I could get it to go away, it seemed, or to please it for a while, by playing my violin. It seemed to wish for me to play, and this I was willing enough to do. Was it a dog or an Indian chief or a crooked tree as it once insisted? I can only say it had a voice. Perhaps it was that only, a voice.

Javier Zamora

To Abuelita Nelly

It's my 14th time pressing roses in fake passports
for each year I haven't climbed marañon trees. I'm sorry
I've lied about where I was born. Today, this country
chose their first black president. Maybe he changes things.
I've told Mamá Paty I don't want to have to *choose*
to get married. You understand. Abuelita, I can't go back
and return. There's no path to papers. I got nothing left
but dreams where I'm: the parakeet nest on the flor
de fuego, the paper boats we made when streets flooded,
or toys I buried by the foxtail ferns. Do you know
the ferns I mean? The ones we planted the first birthday
without my parents. I'll never be a citizen. I'll never
scrub clothes with pumice stones over the big cement tub
under the almond trees. Last time you called, you said
the friends I left think that now I'm from some town
between this Bay and our Estero. And that I'm a coconut:
brown on the outside, white inside. Abuelita, please
forgive me, but tell them, they don't know shit.

Rachel Zucker

Just off the Road near Lynchburg, Virginia

John says, *James Wright says* — [something about
how a poet writing about the landscape is
always writing about himself] — I'm listening
but also standing on a bridge over railroad tracks
& watching some sort of woodchuck or muskrat
or groundhog scurry in & out of the hilly underbrush
so not listening closely *Yeah* I say *It's beautiful here
but I was writing city poems so* ... how can I explain
to John I don't believe he exists don't believe
in Virginia or these horses or houses that tractor
lawnmower small mammal burrowing it is too
incredulous such simultaneous lives I'm not sure
the Earth is round can't perceive that & the hills
of Virginia mean I can't see where I am except
right here *Old* mountains *Old* trees, is what Laurel
said when I asked her why I love this landscape
even though I don't believe it exists even when
I'm standing in it *John* I say *I think James Wright
is full of shit* but I don't say that not even
as a joke not even over the phone I want to say
on this first day of spring our bodies will not
break into blossom I want to tell John I don't
believe in the bucolic or the pastoral I can't
believe it's possible to waste my life